TRAVEL AND ADVENTURE IN TIBET

TRAVEL AND ADVENTURE IN TIBET

Including The Diary of Miss Annie R. Taylor's Remarkable Journey from Tau-Chau to Ta-Chien-Lu through the Heart of the "Forbidden Land"

By

WILLIAM CAREY

GYAN

Published by

GYAN

Gyan Publishing House
5, Ansari Road
Daryaganj, New Delhi-110002
Phone: 011-47034999, 9811692060
E-mail: books@gyanbooks.com

Distribution Network
gyanbooks.com
India, USA, Canada, UK, Australia, France

ISBN: 978-81-212-6857-8 (PB)
First Published, 1902

2nd Impression 2023

Printed at: Gyan Press, Delhi.

TRAVEL AND ADVENTURE IN TIBET
Author: WILLIAM CAREY

TIBETAN CURIOS.

1. Prayer flags. 2. Letter from the Dalai Lama. 3. Prayer-wheel, with enclosure. 4. Brick tea. 5. Tract in Tibetan. 6. Brass image of a demon. 7. Tinder-pouch, flint, and cotton. 8. Lama's seal. 9, 10, 11. Tibetan coins. 12. Tibetan text-cards. 13. Card of the Tibet Prayer Union. 14. Embossed leather bag. 15. Cattle-bell. 16. Chopsticks, knife, and sheath. 17. Notice of Kalimpong Mela. 18. Sprig of aconite. 19. Gospel of John in Tibetan. 20. Tea-bowl. 21. Prayer flags. 22. Silken scarf or "khata." 23. Miss Taylor's diary.

TRAVEL AND ADVENTURE IN TIBET

Including the Diary of Miss Annie R. Taylor's Remarkable Journey from Tau-Chau to Ta-Chien-Lu through the heart of the *Forbidden Land*

By WILLIAM CAREY

WITH SEVENTY-FIVE ILLUSTRATIONS

1902

Preface

IN July, 1899, being ordered north by the doctors, I spent a month in Sikkim, that "wedge" between the "three closed lands," Nipal, Bhutan, and Tibet.

This gave me the opportunity of crossing the Jelep La into Tibet and visiting Miss Taylor at her shop in Yatung. The moment this trip was undertaken, I wanted to know a hundred things of which I was ignorant about the country and the missions besetting its borders. The subject grew with inquiry, and I felt keenly the need of a bright, readable book[1] which should give a picture of the land as a whole, and photograph the present position of the investing forces.

Material for such a work began to come in, and with it a great "find," the original diary of Miss Taylor's astonishing journey in 1892–93. To publish this as part of the first scheme would have been to

[1] It is only right to say that I had not then seen "The Great Closed Land" by Miss Marston. The present volume is cast in a different mould.

spoil the symmetry of the whole. Not to publish it would have been to omit something of the very essence of the story. For the journey stands apart as one of the great deeds of the time, and it has had a unique influence over the expansion of Christian effort on behalf of Tibet. Moreover, it is complete in itself, and can never grow stale. It seemed best, therefore, to print first the diary, along with a general account of the country and its people, and this is the volume now placed in the reader's hands. It will be followed, I hope, by another on the border missions if a sufficiency of interesting details and illustrative drawings and photographs can be had to encourage the attempt.

WILLIAM CAREY.

Dacca, Bengal, India.

Contents

List of Illustrations

Authorities Consulted

MY thanks are due to the principal of Serampore College, the principal and librarian of the Dacca College; Rai Sarat Chandra Dās Bahadur, of Darjiling; Lieut.-Col. H. Bower, of Wei Hai Wei; Miss Stirling, of Scotland; Peter Lindeman, Esq., of Darjiling; and Miss Taylor, of Yatung, for the loan of valuable books, without which this volume could not have been prepared.

The chief authorities consulted are given below: —"Narratives of the Mission of George Bogle to Tibet and of the Journey of Thomas Manning to Lhasa," by Clements R. Markham, C. B., F. R. S.; "Travels in Tartary, Tibet, and China," by M. Huc, translated from the French by W. Hazlitt; "Diary of a Journey Across Tibet," by Capt. Hamilton Bower; "Diary of a Journey through Mongolia and Tibet," by William Woodville Rockhill; "The Buddhism of Tibet," and "Among the Himalayas," by Maj. L. A. Waddell, M. B.; "The Great Closed

Land," by Annie W. Marston; "The Gates of Tibet," by J. A. H. Louis, F. R. G. S.; "Working and Waiting for Tibet," from the German of H. G. Schneider; "Among the Tibetans," by Isabella L. Bishop, F. R. G. S.; "Where Three Empires Meet," by E. F. Knight; "Pioneering in Tibet," by Annie R. Taylor; "Tibet," in the "Encyclopædia Britannica"; papers by various travellers in *The Geographical Journal;* Mr. Rockhill's articles in *The Century Magazine;* the Rev. F. B. Shawe's papers in *The Missionary Review of the World;* and the Rev. Graham Sandberg's article in *The Contemporary Review.*

For many of the illustrations I am indebted to Miss Taylor herself, and for others to the courtesy Lieut.-Col. H. Bower; Maj. L. A. Waddell, LL. D., F. L. S.; the Secretary of the Royal Geographical Society; the secretaries of the Moravian Mission Board and the China Inland Mission; Miss Stirling, Hon. Secretary of the Tibet Prayer Union; Mrs. J. A. Graham, and the Rev. Evan Mackenzie, of Kalimpong, British Bhutan; Messrs. Johnston and Hoffman, of Calcutta, and Mr. Fritz Kapp, late of that city, photographers.

Part I

Adventures in Tibet

CHAPTER I

WHICH CHALKS IN THE OUTLINE

THIS is a book for anybody to read. It is travel and adventure; who will not rise to that? And it is travel and adventure in the hardest of all lands left to explore.

Moreover, there are no technical details. It is not the record of any learned expedition. It is simply the diary of a plucky and resourceful woman who pushed her way, practically alone, through the heart of Tibet, and put down all that happened to her as she went along.

The feat was remarkable and astonishing. Without a companion and without equipment this unsophisticated pilgrim crept into the secret places of the Great Closed Land. Her audacity makes one hold one's breath: what chance has a mouse in a cageful of cats? Others had been before her, but not women. Women have been since, but not alone. There is nothing to equal it in the whole fascinating story of Tibetan travel. Yet how quaintly pathetic in its simplicity and how richly amusing in its unpreparedness!

Starting from the north of China, near the Great Wall, Miss Taylor entered Tibet, penetrated almost to Lhasa, and returned by another route. She was seven months and ten days in the forbidden land. Her only arms were a pistol, and her only instruments a telescope and a watch. The pistol had been packed in the baggage and never saw the light. The telescope was stolen, and it does not appear that she ever had occasion to use it. It was probably intended as a spy-glass for robbers; but those gentry swarmed about her so close and so often that looking for them at long range would have been a mere ridiculous superfluity. The watch she tried unceasingly to barter for something more useful, such as a tent or a tat. Without aneroid, thermometer, or theodolite, she toiled over unmapped mountains and jogged through unvisited valleys, provokingly oblivious of the claims of science, and constrained only when something went wrong with the cooking to notice the boiling-point.

The absence of scientific research does not, however, detract from the human interest of Miss Taylor's story. She kept a diary for the whole period of her adventurous journey, from the day when, at dawn, she stole out of Tau-Chau and across the border, to that other day when she emerged at Ta-chien-lu, having cast her line in a long loop over the rugged interior. This diary is now published for the first time, eight years after the event.

The original lies on my desk. It is a small black notebook, stained and smudged, but closely pencilled on every page. Night after night, at the end of each comfortless march, and as well as numbed fingers would let her, she jotted down the main features of the day. Only those who have faced the cold and fatigue of such travel, without intending to write a book or record the results of scientific observation, can really appreciate the significance of this persistence.

Not till the diary had been written would the tired traveller burrow into her sleeping-bag under tent or cave. When, at last, the tent had been taken, and no cave could be found, she settled herself to sleep on the snow. What a comical little bundle it must have been for the merry stars to wink at!

The steady cheerfulness she exhibited under all circumstances was simply heroic. These blurred pages, what a tale they tell! There is some mention of privations and perils, but how much more that is not mentioned can yet plainly be read in the quivering of the lines and the frequent sunny expressions of hope and trust!

So few travellers have penetrated Tibet, or come back to tell the tale, that their most commonplace experiences are invested with a peculiar interest. The report of Miss Taylor's journey has already gone round the world and excited the admiration of such as know how to estimate intrepid daring and patient, unconquerable courage. To the Christian heart it has spoken in another tone and with thrilling persuasiveness. For there was more in it than mere pluck and perseverance. There was a lofty motive. Mere daring and love of adventure would never have induced this frail woman to hazard her life in such an enterprise, or have carried her so successfully through. It was all that plus an unworldly ideal, a light shining along the path, a fire burning in the bones. It was heroism, but it was also the heroism of faith. The light was "the light of the dark land of Galilee," and the fire a flame from the passionate heart of Paul.

Summaries of the journey already published have made this deep impression. But summaries are far from satisfying. They create a thirst which the meagre information supplied does very little to quench. The mind craves the full story, the detailed happenings of every day, the fresh, original impressions pencilled down on the spot. However crude and imperfect the form in which these are preserved, they are always immensely more interesting than mere general descriptions, the brevity of which deprives them of practical value, while their free coloring is a seductive snare. It is a pity that Miss Taylor's diary was not published at the first, in place of the altogether disappointing and unimpressive accounts which are all that have appeared down to the present time. The narrative, as we find it there, in its wholeness and in its simplicity, is best fitted to form the permanent memorial of a deed which is illustrious in the history of missions and epoch-making for Tibet.

CHAPTER II

THE ENCHANTED LAND

THIS book takes nothing for granted except the general ignorance on so remote a subject. "Where is Tibet?" Miss Taylor was constantly asked as she went among the churches of England and Scotland after her return. Occasionally the wildest guesses were made, some placing it north of the British Isles, some in the heart of Africa, and some amongst the isles of the Pacific.

Nor is this ignorance to be wondered at. In the days when most of us were at school practically the only book on the subject was Huc's "Travels in Tartary, Thibet, and China." And it was a book very variously esteemed. Few, perhaps, ventured to take it seriously. M. Huc might be a charming romancist, but he could scarcely be credited as a sober narrator of facts. His book was not taught in the schools; and Tibet remained simply a blank, or a blind eye, on the maps of the world. Almost all the real exploration of the country has been done in the last twenty years, and the books which have made it popular have been published within a single decade.

Miss Taylor's vivacious jottings open to us the land as it is, with its color and movement as well as its whiteness and weariness, the land as you and I should see it if we went there to-day. And it is not a land easy to get at or easy to see. Not one in a thousand of us is likely ever to see it. We might as well hope to visit the arctic regions and notch our names on the pole!

It is necessary, however, to a proper appreciation of the narrative that some attempt should be made to realize the setting of the story, to understand what was involved in the hard task she set herself to perform. We must know the configuration of the land and its climate, the difficulties presented by its peculiar position and natural characteristics, with the still greater difficulties arising from the spirit of bondage and exclusiveness which broods in the hearts of its people. We must "see a background and feel an atmosphere." We must try to get a "brief vision of the land as a whole."

It can hardly be an exaggeration to say that Tibet is the most forbidding country to be found on the globe. It towers above the clouds the largest and loftiest mass of rock in the world. Hidden behind ramparts of snow and ice, sparsely populated, swept by bitter winds, so cold that the commonest dress of its inhabitants is a huge sheepskin with the wool worn on the inner side: what wonder that its bleak aspect should repel the invader, and make it, in the very heart of Asia and the latitude of the Mediterranean, the least known, the most mysterious area on the surface of the earth?

Round three of its sides, like seas breaking on a rocky coast, rich empires have risen up, rolled on, and disappeared; their thunder booming through the hollow caves, but scarcely heard above the cliff, their foam faintly flecking the black forehead of Tibet. Its people have watched from their high station, with listless eyes, all the procession of the past.

West and south gleamed the painted panorama of the Indian plains, the gilded march of elephants and emperors, the struggle for supremacy of Rajput, Mogul, and Englishman; and it affected little, if at all, the rough race dwelling on the roof of the world. Eastwards seethed the teeming topsy-turvydom of China with a like result. Through all the centuries Bodland[1] stood still, impassive, looking down like some grim image on a grassy green while all this many-colored life bloomed and danced about its feet.

In one matter only has Tibet borrowed from its neighbors. Its wild inhabitants originally

[1] The name by which the country is known to its own people.

worshipped the forces of nature, conceived as destructive demons, and sometimes propitiated with cannibal rites. But now for more than a thousand years there has mingled with this coarse cult the milder faith of Buddha, adulterated by a strong infusion of Hindooism. It came about in a natural and romantic way, the fruit of a marriage between the Tibetan king and two pretty princesses from China and Nipal, who brought their religion with them.

Yet the old demons live and are more powerful than ever. The land is enchanted still and as barbarous as of old,—a land of precious metals without mines;[1] of unlimited resources for trade, but overridden and exploited by brigands; of simple and good-hearted people, but cursed by a mortal terror of malignant spirits, and crushed under the heel of rapacious priests. The newer deities have simply been added to the old. They have not displaced them. The ancient devil-dancer has been superseded by a far more dangerous and powerful oppressor, the magician-priest.

It is the land of the lamas. What that means it

[1] There are certainly mines of a sort in Tibet, but little is known of them. The precious metals are thought to be the treasures of the demons, and are strongly guarded by troops, the diggings being worked only occasionally. "The miners offer sacrifices to the spirits, and then rush to the lodes, and after a few hours rush back again, laden with the spoils of the pick."—"Among the Himalayas."

is not very easy for us, in our Protestant environment, to understand. The lamas are monks. A hundred, or a thousand, or even five thousand, of them may be herded together, if not exactly under one roof, yet in one great building, whose ramifications root themselves like a fortress in the rocks, and whose walls and windows frown upon the surrounding fields. The rest of the timid Tibetans huddle in huts at the monastery gates, or till the soil and tend their flocks that the lamas may live at ease. Deeper than the roots of the lamaseries sink into the rocks has the power of the lamas lodged in the hearts of the people. Every family has at least one representative in the cloisters. Often there are two, and not seldom three. It has been reckoned that every sixth person of the entire population is either a lama or a lama novitiate. The only education is monkish; the only architecture that of the temples and monasteries, which seem to grow out of the craggy heights on which they are perched; the one universal and unceasing religious rite the twirling of a "prayer-wheel" and the mumbling of a meaningless sentence. The lama holds the people in the hollow of his hand, and many forces meet in that magnetic and masterful grip.

A LAMA.

But the chief of all is the weird majesty of the

TYPICAL LANDSCAPE.

A sandy plateau surrounded by high mountains, in Western Tibet.

" Standing in that wild theatre, with his trumpet of human thigh-bone."

land itself. It is a land glittering with gilded temples and fat with green pastures; yet leagues on leagues of it lie with bared bosom to the whistling heavens, white and cold. You may saunter through sunny valleys yellow with ripe corn, and anon paddle in streams whose sands are gold; but there is one background that never alters and that never entirely recedes from view,—that unspeakably solemn horizon of snowy peaks, over which a dazed eagle may flutter in convulsive flight, or the thin black line of trade slowly crawl, dropping its frozen dead. In any other environment the lama would be merely a dirty and revolting pretender. But, standing in that wild theatre, with his trumpet of human thigh-bone at his lips, and a skull in his hands, he is the very embodiment of the spirit that haunts the mountains, and broods over the wide, inhospitable deserts, and makes a sport of man. It is the spirit of awe and mystery that smites the heart with panic and congeals the blood.

And this is the enchantment with which the land is enchanted.

CHAPTER III

CLIMBING THE THRESHOLD

TO climb only to the threshold of this forbidding land means to scale the Himalayas. The Himalayas bulge southwards with a bold sweep, buttressing the Tibetan plateau, and rising from the Indian plains to a height of seventeen thousand feet in a hundred miles. It is the grandest stairway in the world.

The steps of these stairs are separate tiers of mountains, divided from one another by deep chasms which have to be trodden to the bottom before you ascend again. The climb takes a week, and is very toilsome and depressing. You labor for long, hot hours up the steep face of a shelterless ridge, only to scramble down on the other side, lose all you have gained, and begin over again. The terrible gorges between these almost perpendicular walls are death-

A VIEW IN WESTERN TIBET.

traps of fever, being choked with steamy vegetation and excessively hot. Through some of them glacier-fed streams babble over the stony bottom, or race with swift current, creating a cold back draught which chills the blood like the touch of a snake. The heated traveller, gasping for breath, flings himself into a lounge chair on the veranda of some pretty bungalow overhanging the stream, and the next few minutes of blissful coolness may cost him his life.

But the toils of the ascent are rewarded when you reach the summit of the last precipitous cliff, and stand at a dent in the sky-line, and look back over the split escarpment to the far level where the plains shimmer in colored mist. Face north. You are standing on the edge of the outer Himalayan wall, on the crest of the bulge. It is cut into countless peaks like the teeth of a saw, and between the peaks are fearsome glaciers and crevasses unexplored by man. Deeper hollows mark the few passes, the only gates into the country so jealously closed. The pass that we have climbed is one of the easiest and lowest; yet it is nearly as high as Mont Blanc. Before us—all that vast silence of mountains muffled in snow—that is Tibet. Look at it well. Many feet have come as far as this, but no further. Many eyes have scanned with a wistful gaze that strange, solitary prospect. One step more, and you have crossed the threshold; you have passed through the mysterious portals; you have entered the Forbidden Land.

The track wriggles down the steep slope, which here looks as smooth as the blade of a hatchet, till it touches that frozen tarn. All around are rough towers of black, jagged rock. Follow it with your eye till it dips and disappears among the hills. Through the snow on those lower spurs dark pines protrude and stretch their ragged limbs. Far down, seven miles from the pass and four thousand feet below it, deep in a wedge-shaped gorge, that is yet ten thousand feet above the sea, lies the "trade mart," Yatung, where Miss Taylor keeps her famous shop and is still the only missionary allowed to live *in* Tibet.

CHAPTER IV

THE CHANG AND ITS BROKEN EDGE

THE core of Tibet is the Chang. Realize the Chang, and you have the key to everything that is interesting in the history and geography of the land. The Chang is the great plateau, and all the rest of Tibet is its broken edge.

A good idea of the Chang can be gained from the shaded map. It is far from being an accurate delineation, though for the purpose of a rough general view it will serve our turn. The plateau is projected from the north, and pushes evenly westward, filling a knot in the Himalayas with its consistent mass. It originally spread to the great bulge on the south and the Chinese border on the east. But its surface on these two sides has been bitten and fissured and crumbled down from the centre for hundreds of miles by the action of large rivers, the grinding of glaciers, and the scouring of the rains.

The Chang has an astonishing altitude and is comparatively level. Travellers have crossed it in several directions during recent years. Capt. M. S.

Wellby of the Eighteenth Hussars and Mr. Malcolm of the Ninety-Third Highlanders travelled through the country from west to east in the summer of 1896. "For four months," says Captain Wellby, "we saw no vegetation higher than an onion, and for nearly four months our camp was at an average height of sixteen thousand feet. For more than fourteen weeks we travelled without seeing any sign of mankind."[1]

From Leh, on the Indian side, to Tankar, in China, the distance is two thousand miles, and they did it in five months and a half. "Ruby," a little fox-terrier, accompanied them all the way. Generally speaking, the route lay along broad, open valleys, some sixteen thousand feet high, and after every four or five days they would cross an easy pass into another. There was a difficulty about water. The Chang abounds in lakes, some being of great size, but they are nearly all salt. The explorers had to dig several feet for water almost every day. The Tibetan rock salt, which forms a large trade with Nipal and Sikkim, is got directly from these, the purer sort being picked up in large crystals on the wet margin of the beach.[2]

The climate of the Chang is terribly trying. The thermometer will rise to 110° Fahrenheit in the

[1] *The Geographical Journal*, September, 1898.

[2] See Major Waddell's description in "Among the Himalayas."

sun, and sink at night to 25° of frost. This is due to the great rarefaction of the air and the wonderful clearness of the sky. All travellers have noticed the marvellous depth and blueness of the Tibetan heavens. But the biting wind—nothing can keep it out. Blankets and rugs are absolutely useless. Skins alone are adequate as protection, and these must be stout and woolly. Captain Wellby lost nine mules in a single night from the gnawing cold. Mr. St. George R. Littledale, who came over the Chang from the north in 1895, started with a caravan of one hundred and sixty animals, but of all these only two ponies and six mules lived to get back.[1] The extreme dryness of the air produces some painful effects. The mouth, throat, and nostrils get parched, and the skin chaps and cracks. But there are compensations. Meat, for instance, will keep for any length of time. It may powder, but it never putrefies. Miss Taylor sent me the other day some dried ribs of mutton, the flesh of which had shrunk almost to the bone, but had no suggestion of taint, even after crossing the steamy plains of Bengal. She assured me that if first soaked in water, and then cooked, the meat would be found abundant, sweet, and good. I wish now that I had put this to the test instead of sending it as a curiosity to England.

[1] *The Geographical Journal*, May, 1896.

THE PLATEAU PRACTICALLY UNINHABITED

Southward, the Chang extends to the Tengri-Nor, and there encounters the inner wall of the Himalayas, a mighty range which lifts up enormous peaks capped with eternal snow. The whole of this vast region is practically uninhabited. For a brief summer it is one boundless prairie, covered with a thick carpet of grass and flowers, and the happy abode of innumerable herds of wild horses, asses, yak, goat, and antelope. While the summer lasts, a few nomad tribes gather on the edge of the Chang, their flocks nibbling at the fringe of this green felt, till the approach of winter warns them off, and the winds dry up the grass, making it as brittle as bone and as hard as wire. All the rest of the year it is a raw, inhospitable waste, untrodden by the foot of man, yet still mysteriously supporting the hosts of wild animals which survive the arctic cold. Captain Bower, who crossed Tibet in 1891, thinks this can be accounted for only by the amount of fat they lay up when the grass grows at its best.

The typical animal of Tibet is the yak, and its home is on the Chang. In appearance it resembles the ox, but its sides are draped with long, shaggy hair, and its bushy tail is a familiar article of commerce. Set in the horn of an antelope, tipped with silver, it dangles from the sashed waist of many a

" Enormous peaks capped with eternal snow." Page 30.

smart syce on hot evenings in Calcutta. It is both an ornament and a brush for flicking away the flies when the horses stand. Alive, it swept the snow, and whisked about the barren crags of the Himalayas; dead, it adorns a cushioned carriage on the Red Road or the Strand.

The yak is a large, ungainly-looking beast, but the most useful carrier in the country. It is not troubled by palpitations and mountain-sickness, which kill off so many ponies and mules; and it is as sure-footed as the goat. It will carry heavy loads, such as great blocks of salt or bricks of tea, over precipitous places where no other animal could venture and live; and it forges for itself and the caravan behind it a lane through the snow-drifts on the high passes. But it moves slowly and soon gets footsore over stony ground. Its flesh is eaten throughout Tibet. On the Chang it forms the

A YAK.
(Loaded for the march.)

staple food of the nomads. Captain Wellby and Mr. Malcolm boiled down its fat into cakes which they munched like Everton toffee. Its milk is richer than that of the cow, and makes excellent butter, which, however, is preferred when it has become old and rancid. The people flavor their tea with this butter at every meal. Skins of it are buried in the ground and kept for sixty or even a hundred years, to be opened only on state occasions. The Tibetans like their wine fresh and their butter stale.

There is no timber on the Chang and very little anywhere in Tibet. The dried dung of the yak, called jo, forms the principal fuel. It is gathered into great heaps by the nomads and piled round their tents to keep out the cold. The tents are made of the coarse black hair of the same animal, loosely woven. This cloth is much rougher and stouter than sacking, and it looks like matting of tarred cord more than anything else. Yak-hair is also used for a variety of manufactures, including the gauze goggles, hard as wire, which are universally worn for protection against snow-blindness.

The Chang is a monster watershed. Most of the great rivers that shape the maps of India, China, and Burmah flow down from the edge of the Tibetan plateau, and have cut for themselves long, irregular channels reaching far inland. This is especially true of the eastern side, where the configuration of the country, on the map, presents the appearance of a long, skeleton hand, the fingers of which are bent over and pressed down towards the central mass. The valleys and slopes formed by these deep indentations are the chief habitable parts of the country. The rest of the broken portion is precipitous,—a succession of stony ridges and snowy heights, with here and there a level breadth, a lovely glen, or a patch of forest growth. There the rivers take their rise, or the streams spread out over a plain; the ground is marshy and full of pitfalls for man and beast. This is the most rugged and furrowed part of Tibet, and it stretches from the Chinese border to Lhasa. Miss Taylor travelled over it in two directions, and found crossing the rivers only a little less arduous than climbing the mountains between them.

WESTERN TIBET

Westward the Chang is bounded by the Himalayas, and thence descends steeply and swiftly to the plains. There is scarcely any level; it is all bluff cliff and sheer perpendicular rock. The broken edge here includes Ladakh and Baltistan, sometimes called respectively "middle" and "little" Tibet. The scenery is more striking than that of any other part of the country; the rivers are swifter, and all born of the melting of the snow; the herbage is scanty, being only such as can cling to the crags and survive the constant scraping of rubble and snow as these fall over the face of the cliff.

ISKARDO: WESTERN TIBET.

In this region there is practically no rain, but the sky is often coppery and hazy from the immense quantities of fine desert dust blown over from Turkestan. There is no rain, because the central Himalayan chain intercepts the moisture-laden clouds as they come up from the south, leaving all western Tibet a dry and arid land. It is said that only a hundred square miles is cultivated out of an area of more than twenty-one thousand, and this though every available patch is used and many ingenious contrivances are resorted to for the purpose of irrigation. Here is a picture drawn by Mr. Knight: "The mountains that slope to the torrent-bed are perfectly bare and very steep, but nearly half-way up this dreary wall of rock, some thousands of feet above the river, one long, thin, green horizontal line extended as far as eye could see, following for leagues every inequality of the mountain-side round projecting bluffs and retreating hollows."[1] These canals, placed at an almost inaccessible height, must require a great deal of patient labor to construct and keep in repair. The same writer graphically describes the avalanche falling from above and the perils of navigation on skin rafts in the torrent below: "Often we hear a dull roar, and on looking up perceive a great cascade of powdery snow pouring over the high cliff-edge to fall perpendicularly some hundreds of feet, and then swoop down lower mountain-slopes in a succession of white billows to the valley-bottom."[2]

"We found awaiting us a raft of forty goatskins supporting a framework of light sticks. We kept well in the middle of the river, and, as the men had little control over their vessel with their bladeless poles, she was constantly revolving, which enabled me to admire all the scenery round without turning my head. The goatskins leaked a good deal, as was testified to by the constant bubbling and whistling sounds beneath us; but the crew stuck manfully to the pumps. The legs of the inflated goatskins pass upwards between the framework of the raft, and serve as pipes by which the air is

[1] "Where Three Empires Meet," p. 116.

[2] Ibid., p. 268.

replenished. On either side we saw the sands and rocks quivering. The scenery was ever rapidly changing as we flew by. Now a magnificent rocky cape would jut out from the mountains into the foaming breakers; now a long, low promontory of green orchards would shut in a bay of still blue water, forming a charming foreground to the bare hillsides and snowy peaks that rose behind."[1]

A GORGE ON THE WAY TO TS'IN CHAU.

There are good roads through western Tibet, considering the difficult nature of the country. In the side valleys, however, these dwindle to narrow tracks, and are "sometimes carried on precarious scaffoldings along the face of commanding precipices." Many of the streams are

[1] "Where Three Empires Meet," pp. 257–260.

bridged. The Tibetan rope bridge is now pretty well known. "It consists mainly of three cables, one for the feet and one for each hand. These

ROPE BRIDGE NEAR TA-CHIEN-LU.

hang in a deep loop over chasms a hundred or more feet in depth, and sway frightfully. They are repeatedly swept away by avalanche and flood. The transmission of letters is often very uncertain and hazardous. At one place the rope bridge has disappeared. In that case, letters are attached to a stone and thrown across, and naturally not every letter reaches the opposite bank. When despatch is urgent, the sender fastens an eagle's feather to the missive." [1]

The capital of Ladakh is Leh. It stands half-

[1] See article by Rev. James Johnston in *The Christian Commonwealth*, August 31, 1899.

way between the markets of India and those of central Asia. It is therefore the terminus for caravans from both regions. In the summer traders arrive and rest a month or two before going back. They come from Siberia and China and all parts of Tibet, as well as from Turkestan and the plains of Ind. The bazaar is thronged with camels and yaks. Ladakh and Baltistan are no longer parts of Tibet. They belong to the dominions of the Maharajah of Kashmir. But the inhabitants are Tibetans, and so are those of Lahoul and Spiti, two tiny British districts adjoining, which are well known as the headquarters of the Moravian mission.

THE HEART OF THE LAND

Southern Tibet is the populous heart of the land. Here are the chief towns. Here is the sacred city. Here flows the principal river. In summer this zone is sweet and sunny, tinkling with water-music and humming with human life; though in winter, like the rest, it is hard as iron, frost-bound, and crusted with ice.

The great river is the Tsanpo. Rising in western Tibet, it runs eastward for a thousand miles behind the Himalayan walls, and then, suddenly turning south, bursts through them, drops seven thousand feet, and plunges into an unexplored tangle of savage hills, to reappear in Assam. Thence, as the noble Brahmaputra, it bears the freight of a province to Calcutta and the Bay of Bengal. The "unexplored" piece is a length of less than two hundred miles, and determined efforts have been made to see it through, to connect the river above with the river below, and set all doubt at rest. An Indian surveyor, half a Tibetan by birth, almost succeeded, though the savage inhabitants made several attempts on his life, and he suffered terrible hardships. He was commissioned to get as far down as he could, and then to fling into the stream five hundred marked logs of a given shape. This he did; but, owing to an unfortunate failure in the arrangements, no one was sent to watch for them at the other end, and the fruit of his heroic attempt was lost.

The Chang recedes from the southern frontier far inland. Its broken edge on this side bears no resemblance at all to a plateau, the many affluents of the Tsanpo having worn it into numerous easy valleys, which are so many busy roads and avenues to Lhasa, the holy city. But over those roads no foreigner may pass. For this part of the country is more jealously closed and more vigilantly guarded than any other.

CHAPTER V

LHASA: THE HOLY CITY

THE eyes of millions look with longing to Lhasa. As far north as the Volga, and over the whole of Mongolia and Tibet, the mysterious city has cast its spiritual spell. It is six months distant from the homes of some of its devotees, and the journey must be made over the roughest mountains in the world, not to speak of the rigors of the climate and the certainty of falling amongst thieves; yet they perform it with alacrity, even weak women bravely tramping, their packs on their backs, animated by the hope of setting foot in the holy place. Many perish on the road, but those who survive forget their sufferings and count it all joy to have gained the goal.

What is the spell? What is it that speaks home to their hearts? It is not the Lha, though the city is Lha-sa, "seat of the gods." For the Lha, while beings of celestial birth, are busy with their own pleasures in the gardens of bliss, and trouble themselves not at all about the human creatures in this lower world, who may yet some day by force of

LHASA.

merit join their ranks. The Lha are remote and indifferent, however fondly imagined and admired. It is not the Lha, but the Living One, the all-pitiful "Looking-Down Lord" who actually resides in the flesh in his temple-palace at Potala, above the city. This is Avalokita (in Tibetan, Chenraisi), said to be incarnate in the Dalai Lama. The towers of his temple, covered with gold plates, flash in the sun, spreading the beams of his glory, and beckoning his worshippers to come and bask in his smile.

The "Looking-Down One" is painted and imaged throughout Tibet in a variety of forms. Many eyes are given him and many hands, and they all mean compassion. The eyes look down to pity the sufferings of men, the hands are outstretched to help and save. The mere belief that Lhasa was under the special protection of this almighty and compassionate being would have been sufficient to make the city a sweet refuge for the sinful and the distressed. His image, set up in gold or carved in the turret rock, would have drawn thousands of pilgrims and, idealized, have seemed to reflect, even in metal and adamant, some of the divine beneficence. How much more when his very presence is believed to tabernacle on the spot incarnate in human form! Above the seat where he dispenses mercy sits no cold, unimpressionable image of stone, but a breathing body, lithe, warm, and living, a face lighted up with smiles, lips that speak, and hands that are laid with a felt touch of blessing on the worshipper's head. In one word, the city is a shrine, and the Grand Lama is its human idol. The man is a god.

Lhasa has been visited by twenty-two Europeans, almost all of whom were Roman Catholic priests. The first was Friar Odoric, who passed through it in 1325. There was no Grand Lama then. The second, a Jesuit, came three centuries later. There was a fifth Grand Lama then, but he was the first to get the title "Dalai," and to give himself out as an incarnation.

Of all the twenty-two, only one was an Englishman,—Thomas Manning. And it is ninety years since this whimsical traveller entered the city. He was there some weeks, but he made poor use of his unique opportunity. Nevertheless, he enjoyed the distinction of an interview with the Dalai Lama, of which he has left us an interesting account. The date was December 17, 1811.

"We rode to the foot of the mountain on which the palace is built, or out of which, rather, it seems to grow; but, having ascended a few paces to a platform, were obliged to dismount. From here to the hall where the Grand Lama receives visitors, is a long and tedious ascent. It consists of about four hundred steps, partly stone steps in the rocky mountain, and the rest mere ladders from story to story in the palace. Besides this, from interval to interval along the mountain, wherever the ascent is easy, there are stretches interspersed, where the path continues for several paces without steps. At length we arrived at the large platform on which is built the hall of reception. There we rested awhile, arranged the presents, and conferred with the Lama's Chinese interpreter.

"I entered and made the due obeisance, touching the ground three times with my head to the Grand Lama. I presented my gifts, delivering the coin and the handsome silk scarf with my own hands into the hands of the Grand Lama. I then took off my hat, and humbly gave him my clean-shaven head to lay his hands upon. The ceremony of presentation being over, I sat down on a cushion not far from the Lama's throne, and had tea brought to me. It was most excellent, and I meant to have emptied the cup, but it was whipped away suddenly before I was aware of it. The Lama's beautiful and interesting face and manner engrossed almost all my attention. He was at that time about seven years old, and had the simple, unaffected manners of a well-educated, princely child. His face was, I thought, poetically and affectingly beautiful. He was of a gay and cheerful disposition, his beautiful mouth perpetually unbending into a gracious smile which illuminated his whole countenance. Sometimes, particularly when he looked at me, his smile approached to a gentle laugh. No doubt my grim beard and spectacles somewhat excited his risibility. He inquired whether I had not met with molestation and difficulties on the road, to which I promptly returned the proper answer. I said I had had troubles; but, now that I had the happiness of being in his presence, they were amply compensated. I thought of them no more. I could see that this answer pleased both the Lama and his household people. They thus found that I was not a mere rustic, but had some tincture of civility in me. A small present of dried fruits was brought and set before me. They motioned to my servant to take it off, and we withdrew. . . . I was extremely affected by this interview with the Lama. I could have wept through strangeness of sensation. I was absorbed in reflections when I got home."[1]

After Manning, the next, and the last Europeans, to enter the sacred city were the two French fathers, Huc and Gabet. They came from Peking, spent two months in Lhasa, and were then expelled. M. Huc published a delightful account of

[1] For the complete account see "Narratives of the Mission of George Bogle to Tibet and of the Journey of Thomas Manning to Lhasa," by Clements R. Markham, C. B., F. R. S., pp. 258–267.

their travels, profusely illustrated, and subsequently translated into English by Mr. Hazlitt. It contains the only pictorial view of the city which has ever been given to the world.

The travellers reached their destination on January 29, 1846. The last stage was difficult. "Between us and Lhasa there was only a mountain, but this mountain was, past contradiction, the most rugged and toilsome that we had as yet encountered. The Tibetans and Mongols ascend it with great unction, for it is understood amongst them that whoever attains its summit attains a remission of all sins. We had started at one o'clock in the morning; yet it was not till ten in the forenoon that we reached this beneficial summit.

"The sun was nearly setting when, issuing from the last of the infinite sinuosities of the mountain, we found ourselves in a vast plain, and saw on our right Lhasa, the famous metropolis of the Buddhic world. The multitude of aged trees which surround the city with a verdant wall, the tall white houses with their flat roofs and their towers, the numerous temples with their gilt roofs, the Buddha-La, above which rises the Palace of the Talé Lama,—all these features communicate to Lhasa a majestic and imposing aspect."

With this may be compared the description given of the entry, thirty-six years later, of Baboo (now

Rai Bahadur) Sarat Chandra Das, a Bengalese explorer, whose journey from Darjiling to Lhasa and back in 1882 deserves a wider recognition.

"Our hero was now not one day's journey from Lhasa. Classical sites abounded on every hand. Travelling rapidly across an extremely fertile-looking plain, Daipung Monastery was passed away to the left, and then the towers and glittering pinnacles of the sacred city soon burst upon the view. Here, at length, was the object of all his dreams and of all his arduous adventures, lying sedately before him on the open plain! Lhasa the mysterious, the home of occult learning, the abode of the hierarch of all Buddhism, was reached, visibly reached, at length. It was four o'clock in the afternoon as he approached the western gate of the city. Carefully did he arrange his garments, and, having permitted his attendants to adjust his waist-sash exactly as an orthodox Tibetan gelong's (lama's) should be tied, he formed his party into a small procession after the manner of the newly arrived. With a small banner streaming from the head of a pike carried over the shoulder of the man who walked first, with his beasts and other servants following next, and with himself bringing up the rear, drooping wearily on his pony,—thus did Sarat Chandra Das enter bravely the gateway of the unknown city of Lhasa.

RAI SARAT CHANDRA DAS BAHADUR,

The intrepid Indian traveller, who visited Lhasa, and had an interview with the present Dalai Lama in 1882.

"No one offered to molest the party as they made their way through the main street of the outer city. As Chandra Das wore colored goggle spectacles, and looked somewhat of a general wreck, the loungers freely remarked upon his appearance. 'Another sick man,' exclaimed an idler at a Chinese pastry-shop door; 'why, the city will soon be full of such.' They afterwards learned that smallpox was already spreading in epidemic form through Lhasa. A ride of half a mile brought the party to the inner gate of the city. Here watchmen were stationed, but they barely glanced at the newcomers, who sedately filed through the portal, and found themselves now, apparently so simply and easily, in the very heart of the place which had once seemed so far off and so impossible to attain to. The attendants of the baboo, who were in his secret, now advised him to turn into a side lane while they went in search of lodgings. On their return, the baboo, who had been submitting to some catechetical inquiries from casual passers-by, was hurried into a network of filthy lanes, under a dark archway, and, climbing a ladder in an inner court, was duly introduced to his suite of apartments. The date of his arrival was May 30."[1]

To another Indian explorer, "A. K.," we are

[1] Rev. Graham Sandberg in *The Contemporary Review*, July, 1890.

indebted for a carefully drawn plan of the city. When the Tibetan authorities in 1865 refused to allow Europeans to enter the country, the Indian government trained and equipped a number of native surveyors, of Tibetan extraction, and sent them across the Himalayas to map out the land.

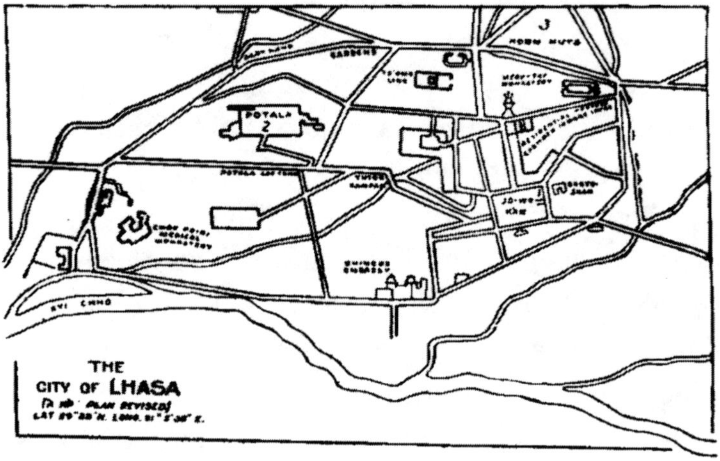

PLAN OF LHASA.

1. Jo-wo K'an ("the Lord's house"), the cathedral of Lhasa.
2. Potala, palace of the Dalai Lama.
3. Horn Huts.

Their reports form the basis of nearly all our knowledge of southern Tibet. "A. K." spent a year in the capital, and secretly measured with his rosary every street in the place.

The houses of Lhasa are whitewashed without and dirty within. The material used is mud and sun-dried brick or stone. Bands of yellow or red, the two ecclesiastical colors, are painted round the doors and windows. The rooms have an open sky-light to carry off the pungent smoke of the argols, which are burned in a glazed vessel on the floor.

In the western suburbs there are some curious dwellings built entirely of the horns of oxen and sheep. "The horns of the oxen being smooth and white, and those of the sheep, on the contrary, rough and black, these various materials are susceptible of infinite combinations, and are arranged accordingly, in all sorts of fantastic designs; the interstices are filled up with mortar. These houses are the only buildings that are not whitewashed."

The main streets are broad and clean, but the outskirts and byways are "revoltingly filthy," despite the many gardens which give it such an attractive appearance.

The palace-temple of Potala is a mile from the city gates, and approached by a fine avenue of trees. There is a constant peregrination of pilgrims both here and around the wall of the cathedral, beginning with gun-fire from the Chinese embassy at 4 A. M., and closing at 9 P. M., when the same gun is fired as the signal for retiring to rest.

The cathedral stands on the site of the original temple built by King Sron Tsan Gampo for the accommodation of the wondrous images brought him by his Buddhist wives. It stands in the centre of the city, and is a colossal structure. The entrance faces the east. Before it stands a flagstaff forty feet high, adorned with yak's hair and horns of yak and sheep. The main building has three stories and is roofed with plates of solid gold. The interior is dark. There are three long and two cross aisles. The light comes from above over the middle and broadest aisle, where a transparent oilcloth serves instead of glass. Through this alone can daylight enter the temple. There are no side windows. The cathedral contains fifteen plates of massive silver, covered with innumerable precious stones. The image of Buddha, given by the Chinese emperor, with his daughter, to King Sron Tsan Gampo, is of gigantic proportions and richly gilded. Flowers are daily showered upon it. The wings of the building are divided into cloisters, lecture-rooms, and residences for officials, with a special apartment for the Dalai Lama.[1]

But the real centre of Lhasa, the beating heart of Tibet, is not the cathedral within the walls, but the palace of Potala without. It is true that pilgrims bring flowers to the great image in the cathedral, but they fall into a lap of stone, and are wasted on those hard knees. They offer prayers, but the image cannot hear. They gaze in adoration, but no answering look comes from those ab-

[1] Waddell's "Buddhism of Tibet," pp. 300, *et seq.*

stracted eyes. Then they go out to Potala, climb up the steeps of the holy hill, and are ushered into the presence of a god who can see and listen, and visibly bestow a blessing.

The following is an interesting account by "A. K." of an ordinary reception there:—

"Since his worshippers are in thousands, and it is only to those who are wealthy or of high degree that he can afford to address even a brief sentence or two, this is always done in a deep, hoarse voice, acquired by training in order to convey the idea that it emanates from maturity and wisdom. Seated cross-legged on a platform some six feet high, he is dressed to be worshipped in the usual colors of priesthood, red and yellow, and with bare arms, and holds a rod from the end of which hangs a tassel of silk, white, red, yellow, green, and blue. The pilgrim, coming in, advances with folded hands as if in prayer, and, resting his head against the edge of the platform above him, mentally and hastily repeats the petitions he would have granted. The Dalai Lama is understood to comprehend intuitively; he touches the pilgrim's head with the bunch of silk in token of his blessing, and the worshipper is hurried out of the east door, only too happy if he has passed say half a minute in the presence. Persons of rank or substance are permitted to mount the platform and to perform obeisance there, receiving the required blessing by actual touch of the Dalai Lama's hand."

Sarat Baboo attended a more select reception, given by the present Dalai Lama when he was eight years old.

"We were seated on rugs spread in about eight rows, my seat being on the third row, at a distance of about ten feet from the Grand Lama's throne, and a little to his left. There was perfect silence in the grand hall. The state officials walked from left to right with serene gravity, as becoming their exalted rank in the presence of the supreme vicegerent of Buddha on earth. . . .

"The great altar, resembling an Oriental throne pillared on lions of carved wood, was covered with costly silk scarfs; and on this his holiness, a child of eight, was seated. A yellow mitre covered the child's head, his person was robed in a yellow mantle; and he sat cross-legged, with the palms of his hands joined together to bless us. In my turn I received his holiness's benediction and surveyed his divine face. I wished to linger a few seconds in the sacred presence, but was not allowed to do so, others displacing me by pushing me gently. . . . When all were seated after receiving benediction, the head steward poured tea into his holiness's golden cup from the golden teapot. Four assistant servers poured tea into the cups of the audience. Before

THE DALAI LAMA ON HIS THRONE.
By a Chinese Artist.
(This is said to be "very like him" by one who has seen him often.)

the Grand Lama lifted his cup to his lips a grace was solemnly chanted. We slowly lifted our cups to our lips and drank the tea, which was of delicious flavor. Thereafter the head butler placed a golden dish full of rice in front of his holiness, which he only touched; and its contents were then distributed. I obtained a handful of this consecrated rice, which I carefully tied in one corner of my handkerchief. After grace had been said, the holy child, in a low, indistinct voice, chanted a hymn. . . . Then a venerable gentleman rose from the middle of the first row of seats, and addressing the Grand Lama as the Lord Chenraisi incarnate, recited the many deeds of mercy which that patron saint of Tibet had vouchsafed towards its benighted people. At the conclusion he thrice prostrated himself before his holiness, when a solemn pause followed, after which the audience rose, and the Grand Lama retired."[1]

In the spring of the year Lhasa holds high carnival, and is given up to games, tumbling, archery contests, putting the stone, rope-walking, masquerades and religious processions. The head of the De-pung Monastery then rules for a month. He comes to the city, and is given a royal reception. Prisoners are released, and there is much rejoicing. But many weep, for, assisted by thirty deputies, he

[1] "Buddhism in Tibet," pp. 322, 323.

sets about hunting up trifling offences and inflicting heavy fines. In this manner the De-pung treasury is enriched. In order to avoid the fines, the people of Lhasa whitewash their houses annually before the arrival of this temporary king.

During that festival month the city is red with monks. They come from far and near, to the number of thirty thousand, and quarter themselves within the walls. Devotees go round the temples, measuring their length on the ground; and women, for the only time in the year, are allowed to enter the monasteries. Imposing processions, led by all the civic authorities, sing their way to the cathedral, while attendants distribute largess, such as little bits of brick tea, etc., to the excited crowds. Inside, the cathedral is a blaze of color and light. There are four hundred images to be worshipped, and "round the holiest of these thousands perform solemn circuits, often upon their knees." At night ten thousand lamps illumine the building.

In connection with these lamps, which are vessels of butter constantly replenished by the pilgrims, a pretty story is told.

A poor old widow from a distant part of Tibet came on pilgrimage to see and worship the great image of "the Lord" at Lhasa. When she reached the city, her little store was exhausted, and she had nothing to offer. But she begged a morsel of butter, and, carrying it to the temple, offered it as a tiny lamp. The Lord revealed himself, and thanked her for her gift, and spoke comfortingly to her. This fact was noised abroad and a rich merchant heard it. He reasoned that, if the Lord had appeared to a woman who offered him only one lamp, he would certainly appear to the donor of many. Whereupon he set out for the temple, and offered thousands of lamps with tons of butter; but the idol remained impassive and unresponsive.[1]

Lhasa is the seat of many manufactures. There are dyers of cloth; and preparers of the perfumed incense sticks, which diffuse an exquisite odor; and workers in the precious metals; and moulders in brass, all busily employed in the streets and shops. And the things they make are stamped with the seal of a special sanctity, the impress and authority of the holy place. For Lhasa is wholly given up to one thing,—religion, and to one act,—worship. It is a mystic casket curiously wrought, and the Dalai Lama is its living jewel.

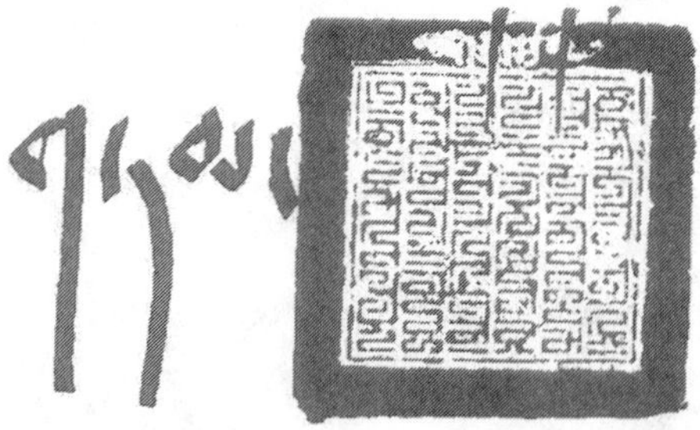

SEAL OF THE DALAI LAMA PUT AT THE HEAD OF HIS LETTERS.

[1] "Buddhism in Tibet," p. 319.

But the Dalai Lama is himself simply a cushioned captive—patted, like the toy, to spend his days in benignant motions, and not seldom poisoned to end them when it is convenient that he should disappear. Till he comes of age—and he does not always come of age—the secular power lies in the hands of another. When he dies, his

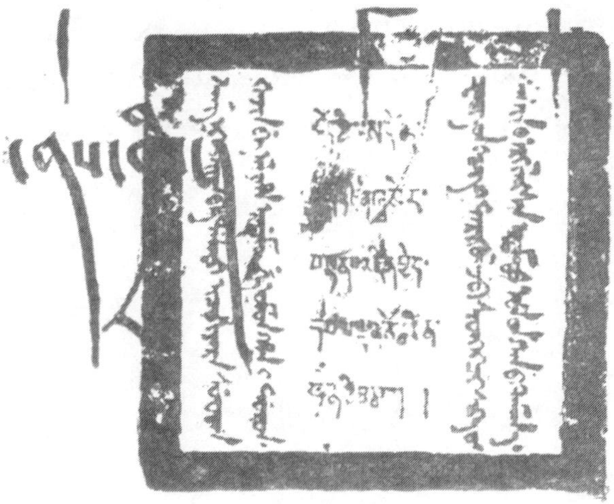

SEAL OF THE DALAI LAMA STAMPED AT THE END OF HIS STATE LETTERS.

body is embalmed, and gold and jewels of a fabulous value are set in his face. Nine months later, search is made for the child, it may be of poor and obscure parents, in whose person he is said to be re-incarnated for the benefit of mankind. Marks and tokens are discovered, and at a suitable age the chosen child is tested by being called upon to point out the rosary and other little personal properties of the late Lama, from amongst a mixed collection. If he is able to do this, he is taken to Lhasa, and to the palace, installed as the Dalai Lama, and worshipped like his predecessor. Thus the regent strengthens his rule, and the wheel of life revolves till a new tragedy occurs.

It will be seen that the holy city is more than the home of metaphysical mysteries and the mummery of idol-worship; it is a secret chamber of crime; its rocks and its roads, its silken flags and its scented altars, are all stained with blood.

CHAPTER VI

TWO SLEEPLESS DOGS

"The Tibetan mastiff is the finest watch-dog in the world. He prowls round the house and is a terror to all travellers."

EVERY p'yling, or foreigner, is excluded from Tibet. The Indian pundits were able to assume disguises impossible to Europeans; but even they crept into the country with their lives in their hands, and had many narrow escapes. As to Europeans, every adventurer who has got into the land since Manning has promptly been escorted out again, sometimes with scant ceremony, and always with a firmness and finesse not to be successfully resisted. In one recent and remarkable instance[1] torture was applied. In another,[2] the unwary traveller was done to death. In a third[3] he disappeared.

Let us try to understand the reasons for this exclusiveness.

Two persons watch the border with sleepless

[1] That of Mr. A. Henry Savage Landor. See "In the Forbidden Land," 2 vols., 1899.

[2] M. De Rhins, June, 1894. See article by Col. Sir T. H. Holdich, in *The Geographical Journal*, February, 1899.

[3] The missionary, Mr. Peter Rijnhart, September, 1898.

eyes. One is a Chinaman, and the other a lama. The lama guards his monopoly in religion, and the Chinaman his monopoly in trade.

With the lama it is obviously a question of life and death. His power is based on the ignorance and superstition of the people, who believe themselves, apart from him, at the mercy of cruel and ubiquitous demons, and therefore requisition his services on every possible occasion, whatever the cost. He is careful to foster this belief, and not to sell his intercession at too cheap a price. It is not to be expected that he should welcome the introduction of more enlightened views; still less, permit the representatives of a rival faith to contest his sway. The opening of the country to travellers and to missionaries would of course tend to dissipate the delusions on which his authority rests, and so to cut short his career. It is the instinct of self-preservation that excites him to fierce opposition, and moves him to drive forth the intruder, and to lock and bolt the doors.

With the Chinaman it is partly a question of political supremacy. He is no less anxious than the lama, and no less angry; but he is far more able and far more quiet. Some assert that he is the real master of Tibet, and there are facts which go far to support such a contention. He is always alert and present at the critical moment, though he prefers to keep in the background at other times. He is sinuous and insincere. He will write you a passport, commanding all men everywhere to meet you with submission and assist you to the full extent of their power, under penalty of the serious displeasure of the emperor; and he will seal this document officially, and place it in your hands with every profession of friendliness and support, only to seal another and despatch it by secret courier, the moment your back is turned, conveying exactly opposite instructions, ordering the people to stop you, turn you back, and put every obstacle in your path.[1] He maintains an amban, or resident, at Lhasa, and his mandarins are stationed in all large towns. The gates of the country, even on the Indian side, are guarded by his soldiers, and it is he who concludes treaties with foreign powers. He is a prominent figure, especially on the trade routes, up and down the land, and a privileged person wherever he goes. He affects to despise the people. He is the porcelain; they are but common clay. And in many parts they yield him the homage he is forward to claim.

For all these reasons it is better to travel with a Chinaman than with mere Tibetans. One Chinaman is equal, as an escort, to three Tibetans; yet,

[1] See Mr. Littledale's experience, *The Geographical Journal*, May, 1896.

for the same reason, if he turns against you, you will have the utmost difficulty in getting your rights respected and bringing him to book. His delinquencies are certain to be winked at, and what redress has a p'yling in a land where his presence is detested?

A p'yling has no rights. As a p'yling you are simply an unwelcome intruder, and the blunt fact to be reckoned with is this, that you ought not to be there. These remarks will find ample illustration in the course of Miss Taylor's story.

I am anxious to express a just judgment with regard to this vexed question of Chinese control. The authorities are not entirely at one. It will be well to give examples. Maj. L. A. Waddell, in his recent beautiful book, "Among the Himalayas," makes the following remarks:—

"For this policy of an exclusion more rigorous than ever, the Chinese excuse themselves by alleging that it is all the doing of the lama priests at Lhasa. But it is the Chinese themselves undoubtedly who are at the bottom of it all, and they merely make a cat's paw of the lamas. The Tibetans are not unfriendly to Europeans, and the lamas least of all wish the trade to be tied up, as they themselves are the chief traders of the country. China, on the other hand, wishes to keep the Tibetan markets to itself, as well as to consolidate its political power there; and its sinister influence at Lhasa in instigating the Tibetans against us on every opportunity has been clearly manifest from the time of Huc downwards."[1]

A still greater authority on things Tibetan is Mr. W. W. Rockhill, late United States minister at Peking, a scholar equally at home in Chinese and in Tibetan literature, and one of the greatest of modern explorers in the Forbidden Land. In his "Diary of a Journey through Mongolia and Tibet"[2] (1891–1892), Mr. Rockhill writes:—

"The Chinese in Tibet do not want to risk their popularity with the dominant class of the country (*i. e.*, the lamas) by befriending foreigners, to do which they would have to assert their authority without any advantage to themselves. Whenever China sees the necessity of doing so, it can effectually assert its supremacy in Tibet, for it is absurd to say that China is not the sovereign power there and that Chinese officials are only there to manage their own people, and are tolerated, as it were, in the country. History, since the time of K'ang-hsi, or Ch'ien-lung, at all events, and also recent events at Lhasa and along the Indian border, prove conclusively that this is not so; but China does not propose to hold

[1] "Among the Himalayas," Westminster: Archibald, Constable, & Co, 1899.

[2] Published by the Smithsonian Institute, Washington, 1894.

Tibet by force of arms—the game would hardly be worth the candle; it is by diplomacy, by superior knowledge of foreign affairs and nations, and by conciliating the lamas, that it preserves its undoubted sway."[1]

On the other side, I have been favored with the following opinion by Lieut.-Col. H. Bower, First Chinese Regiment, who crossed Tibet from Ladakh to China during the same period.

"My own impression is that the Chinese suzerainty is very shadowy, though the Tibetans in exclusiveness are quite willing to take shelter behind the Chinese in negotiations with foreign powers. If China really has power in Tibet, and if it is a part of China, then by the treaty of Tien-tsin, Englishmen can go there on passport, but every one knows that the Chinese are not in a position to issue a passport which the Tibetans would consider valid."

Whether or not the Chinese have all the political influence that is claimed for them, they have certainly a large interest in trade. Tibet is a land of traders. The lamas more than the laity, and the women as much as the men, give themselves in their leisure to commerce. And it is commerce chiefly conducted by barter. There is a Lhasa coinage. But the country is divided into provinces and sub-

[1] "Diary of a Journey Across Tibet," pp. 324, 325.

divided into numerous tribal or territorial sections, some of which are under the government of Lhasa, some directly under China, and others lawless and independent. The notorious Goloks, for instance, have never been subdued. They live by brigandage, and glory in it, periodically raiding their neighbors. The tribes peacefully settled around them sit in constant fear of attack, and, when the raid takes place, offer a feeble resistance, or trek in confusion to more distant fields. The people of one district are often at enmity with the people of another, and this internal state of unrest and uncertainty acts injuriously against any common medium of barter or exchange. Silver and gold, in the raw state, the Indian rupee, and a silver coin called the tanka (worth about sixpence) are pretty generally current. But over large areas some special commodity is made the standard of value; for example, a pair of boots, a brick of tea, a yak-tail, or a length of cloth.

A TANKA.

Tibet is a barren land, and therefore dependent on other countries for most of its food-supplies. But it is rich, and well able to buy all it needs. Its inexhaustible wealth of gold and turquoise, salt, borax, yak-tails, and musk attracts the merchandise of distant nations, not simply to its borders, but over the snowy passes and across stony solitudes to the very centre of its icy circle. The annual caravans, one from each side, work their way over well-worn and time-honored routes, into which run tributary rills of local trade, so that from every town on the borders a road starts for Lhasa.

There is traffic with Mongolia for leather and saddlery; with China for tea, silk, and hardware; with Sikkim and Bhutan for rice and tobacco; and with India generally for broadcloth, indigo, sugar, and spice.

The Chinese control this trade. They guard the passes and levy oppressive, and in some cases prohibitive, customs on imports from other lands. They have practically the monopoly in two most important commodities,—tea and silk.

The Tibetans consume immense quantities of tea. Thousands of camels from Mongolia, and a still larger number of yaks from the Chang, come down every year to carry up the tea. One of the highways through the country is called the "Tea Road." What tea they get from China is poor stuff at the best, being excessively coarse. It is pressed, with the stalks and stems, into solid bricks, which are afterward sewed up in skins. The size varies a little, but an average brick will weigh about eight pounds.

Poor as the tea is, the Tibetans could not live

without it. Mixed with butter and tsamba, or barley-flour (the suttoo of India), it forms the staple food of the country.

Many housewives keep the pot boiling all the day. In some parts a sort of stock solution is prepared, the tea being boiled with soda for several hours, till all its strength is extracted, and then the liquid is strained off and kept. A little of this solution is added to each fresh brew of tea while it lasts. Ordinarily the process is this: A handful of brick tea is taken from the leather bag and put into the pot. Butter, always rancid, is added, and the liquid is boiled for about ten minutes. Then it is strained, and afterward churned in a bamboo tube by means of a wooden disc worked up and down; and finally the beverage thus cooked is poured out into small wooden bowls.

Every Tibetan carries, in the folds of his ample robe or sheepskin, one or more of these little cups, and also his own bag of tsamba, from which he thickens the liquid according to his taste. The bowl is replenished with tea again and again, until he has had enough. Then he invariably licks it clean before replacing it in his bosom. It is never washed. Neither is he. His greasy fingers are merely rubbed on his hair or drawn across his gown. Rich and poor alike eat this common food out of this common cup. The cup is made of red wood from the root of a tree, but it is sometimes lined with silver and so richly ornamented as to cost twenty or thirty pounds.

The trade in tea was formerly accelerated, and is still to some extent, by compulsory sale. The Chinese officials forced a certain quantity on their subordinates; and they, in turn, forced it on the people of their respective districts. Mr. Rockhill found that soldiers were made to accept it in lieu of pay. All this means a rich revenue to China, and practically she has no competitor. For the Indian passes are closed by prohibitive rates. Otherwise, undoubtedly, Indian tea would find a ready and illimitable market in Tibet. It could safely be trusted, on its own merits, to take the place of the rubbish that comes from China. And the cost of transport would be trifling in comparison. From Darjiling to Lhasa by the Jelep-La is a journey of less than three weeks. From the Chinese frontier it is seldom less than six months. Moreover, the region to be crossed on that side is execrably rugged, and yak caravans are slow. On the other hand, it has to be remembered that the people are impressed by officials for food and labor, and this reduces the cost. With such abuses put down, and a fair field, the days of the Chinese monopoly would be numbered. Our yellow brother has reason to be anxious, and his alertness is not surprising. It is no small danger that threatens his trade in tea. It is nothing less than extinction.

Then there is silk and cotton cloth. Cotton is the currency over a wide tract, and it all comes from China. Silk is in enormous demand. The Buddhist sentiment against the taking of life prevents the Tibetans from rearing silkworms for themselves, and China supplies the lack. In the form of a ceremonial scarf (k'atag) it is universally used, and is the recognized and indispensable medium of social intercourse. It must be offered and exchanged on all social occasions. Friend gives it to friend. A stranger presents it when he calls. It is the preliminary sign of civility in conducting negotiations. It is sometimes used as the wrapping of a letter, and finally it is the leading-string by which the lama conducts the corpse to burial. The k'atag is an oblong piece of white or pale blue silk, very thin, almost gauzy in texture, folded like a handkerchief, and much frayed at the ends. Its value varies according to quality and size. It may delicately convey a compliment. It may also insinuate a slight. When you start on a journey, you provide yourself with an assorted supply of these silken symbols suited to the several exigencies of life.

It would be a happy thing if the custom of ceremonial presentation were confined to the offer of k'atags. On the contrary, it includes every portable commodity from a teacup to a tent. You must call on the chief of every town or tent settlement you pass and present him with the best you have. It does not at all follow that you will get an equivalent in return. He will give you something, but it may be the merest trifle; is it not supplemented by his superior rank? Every official in the country has to be propitiated, either to let you alone or to help you along. And this is how it happens that the box or package marked "Presents for Chiefs" is one of the most necessary items in the Tibetan traveller's kit.

But, bribe as you will, you cannot progress beyond a certain stage. The jealous guards dog your steps and keep sleepless watch. We can understand the reason. We have looked into their hearts. The wealth of Tibet is conducted, by a thousand secret and open channels, first, to "those immense reservoirs" the lamaseries; and second, over the frontier, into the great coffers of China. Why should foreigners be suffered to divert the streams?

CHAPTER VII

THE DAWN AND DEVELOPMENT OF LAMAISM

LAMAISM, the religious system taught and practised by the lamas, is peculiar to Tibet. There it is called simply "The Religion" or "Buddha's religion." But, as we have seen, it is Buddhism on a dark ground,—the old dread of demons, and Buddhism in a fancy dress—beflowered and bejewelled by Hindoo forms of polytheistic faith. In a word, it is the lotus blooming on a black and sullen sea, the Ganges flowing through Greenland.

The word "lama" means "superior," and is pure Tibetan. It should properly be applied only to heads of monasteries and priests of the higher ranks. But it has come to be used loosely as a general appellation for all members of the monastic order.

Lamaism took a thousand years to develop, and there are seven well-marked stages of growth.

I

First of all, there was the introduction of Buddhism (A. D. 638–641), by the two princesses from China and Nipal. Buddha had been dead eleven hundred years when his name and fame were thus carried into the snowy kingdom. But the young king, Sron Tsan Gampo, to please his wives, sent for books and teachers from the three Buddhist lands. He also built costly temples in which to enshrine the images which they brought with them as part of the marriage dowry. The earliest temple was erected at Ra-sa (red place), subsequently changed to Lha-sa (place of the gods). The messenger sent to India spent several years in that country, studying the sacred books, visiting places of pilgrimage, and imbibing the spirit of Buddhism in its then developed form. He returned to Tibet with many trophies of diligence and much spoil in the shape of books and implements of worship. He also invented an alphabet modelled on that of the Sanskrit, by means of which he reduced the Tibetan language to writing, and translated many of the sacred books. That was the beginning.

II

But the new religion was vehemently opposed by the guardians of the older demonolatry, and for a century it gained little ground. There was no compromise between them. They had nothing in common, and the one hated the other. The doctrines of Buddha are a mild and gentle light fitted to tame a little the wild beast in the heart of man, but utterly powerless to scare away evil spirits or to quench the fear that clutches the soul of their victims. Something much stronger was needed to cope with these terrible foes,—a spell potent and perceivable; a priest, and a priest who should be a magician.

These conditions were fulfilled when the century had run its course. From having been the cult of a feeble and scarcely tolerated sect, the new faith at one bound leaped into popular esteem and spread all over the country. The power to fight the spirits was found, or at any rate professed; and the magician appeared. Thereafter it was no more Buddhism *versus* demonism, but Buddhism absorbing demonism and taking on an entirely new complexion in the process. It was, strictly speaking, no longer Buddhism at all. Buddhism had become Lamaism. This is the second stage of development and the most interesting and important of all. Let us see by what steps it was reached.

The transition was effected by one man, a man whose name is said to be as much honored in Tibet as that of Buddha himself. This man was a celebrated Indian pundit and professor of magic, who lived on the borders of Kashmir. His name was Padma-sambhava.

Padma-sambhava was invited to Tibet by the

reigning king, and he arrived in the year 747. His great reputation as a wizard had preceded him, and he was welcomed with open arms by the superstitious people. The king's idea seems to have been that the pundit should formulate a plan, or establish a régime, by which the still unpopular Buddhist faith might acquire force and influence. Padmasambhava addressed himself to the task with an insight that amounted to genius and a zeal that carried everything before it. He began by marching up and down in the land, ostentatiously working his spells and proclaiming the demons vanquished.

With some of them he appears to have had tough encounters. One demon tried to squeeze him between two mountains, but the sage adopted the simple expedient of soaring, and so escaped. Another hailed thunderbolts at him from her house of snow, but he caused the snow to melt and become a lake. She plunged into the lake for refuge, but he caused it to boil. The flesh was boiled off her bones; still she would not come out. Then he threw in his *dorje*,[1] and pierced her right eye, whereupon she came out and offered him her life-essence. A third spirit assumed the form of a huge white

THE DORJE.
(Every lama carries one.)

[1] A symbolic instrument, signifying thunderbolt, not unlike a dumb-bell. It is the lama's badge and most powerful weapon.

yak, and furiously charged the saint. The pundit simply made some passes in the air, and lo! the brute was hypnotized, bound fast as with cords by nose, neck, and feet! Then it became transformed into a beautiful boy dressed in white silk, who also offered him his life-essence.

Perambulating the country, and performing such prodigies as these, Padma-sambhava rapidly created immense prestige for himself and the disciples who began to flock to his side. He did not make the mistake of ignoring the demons, much less of denying their existence. On the contrary, he magnified their importance and power, their malignant cunning and ruthless rage. He hunted them in their separate haunts, proved himself their match and their master, and then spared their lives on the mutually agreeable understanding that they should adopt the Buddhist religion and he should secure for them in perpetuity the service and worship of the people. That was the great secret of the pundit's plan. It conserved the old faith. Demon-worship was not denounced. It was declared to be necessary, while at the same time it was shown to be futile without the intervention of a priest. The demons were recognized as rampant and irresistible save in the presence of the sage and those to whom he communicated his power.

The magician's policy was adroit and entirely

successful. Within two years after his arrival in the country he had founded the first order of monkish priests, the lamas of to-day, and erected the first monastery in Tibet. This was the monastery at Sam-yas, about thirty miles southeast of Lhasa. Parts of the original building are still standing after eleven hundred and fifty years. Its singular distinction, as prior to all the rest, gives it great importance; and its images, as well as many of its sacred vessels, are said to be of solid gold. A curious relic of the old charmer's influence is found in the firmly rooted belief that this monastery is specially safe and suitable as a repository of treasure. In fact, the Tibetan government is understood to use it as a bank.

Padma-sambhava had twenty-five disciples, whom he instructed in many things besides magical arts. He was warmly backed by the king in all his plans, and several other monasteries soon began to spring up. Finally the great wizard-abbot left Tibet to make similar conquests in other lands. His departure was glorious. Multitudes had gathered to bid him farewell. A rainbow halo was seen to encircle his head, and a celestial chariot bore him through the sky. The people followed him with straining eyes, but they had no need to hurry. They had time to encamp for many days at the foot of a pass while the saint and his party slowly sailed through the heavens, leaving behind them a burning trail like that of a comet or a shooting star.

Lamaism, thus firmly established, grew great and strong. Fresh scholars and sages found their way to Tibet, much encouraged by the lavish patronage of the king. More Indian books were translated into Tibetan, and a splendid dictionary was compiled of Sanskrit-Tibetan terms. But all the time there was an undercurrent of dissatisfaction and revolt. The old Bon priests, representatives of the dragon-worship, resented the usurpation by the lamas of their place and power; and a band of purer Buddhists from China recoiled at the admixture of sorcery with the Buddhist law. Thus passed the second period, lasting a hundred and fifty years.

III

The third crisis came in 899, when the reigning monarch, a generous patron of the lamas, was treacherously murdered at the instigation of his younger brother. This younger brother, whose name was Lan Darma, seized the throne and set himself the task of exterminating lamaism, root and branch. For three years he desecrated the temples, spoiled the monasteries, and burned the sacred books.

At the end of that time he himself was in turn

assassinated. A lama, disguised as a dancer, riding on a black horse and concealing a bow and arrow in his ample sleeves, appeared one evening at the gates of Lhasa. He dismounted and danced before the palace, and danced so well that he was summoned to an audience with the king. During the interview he suddenly snatched out his weapon, and shot Lan Darma through the heart. In the hubbub that ensued the assassin fled from the palace, mounted his steed, and galloped to the nearest stream. The horse, which had been blackened with soot, came out white after fording the river, and his rider escaped. The lamas canonized this deliverer of the church, and soon regained the prestige they had lost. Thus ended that brief period of royal persecution which marks the third epoch in the history of the lamas.

IV

Another century passed. The monks multiplied and grew fat. Monasteries sprang up like magic. But prosperity brought in its train laxity of life and morals, and extravagance of doctrine. Then came the reformation. And the reformation is the fourth act in the Tibetan drama.

The reformer was the great pundit Atisa. Born in Bengal, he travelled to Tibet at the advanced age of sixty, in A. D. 1038. There he wrote many books, and founded the "Reformed Sect" of lamas, out of which grew the Ge-lug-pa, or present established church, three and a half centuries later. Atisa died near Lhasa after fourteen years of fruitful labor in the lamas' land.

V

We now take a double step forward, two hundred years, to the days of the Chinese emperor Kublai Khan. The grandfather of Kublai Khan was the illustrious Mongol monarch Genghis Khan, who conquered Tibet. Kublai added China to these inherited dominions. He was a most enlightened ruler, and anxious to discover some form of religion that should "weld together the more uncivilized portions of his almost unwieldy empire." It is an interesting story. He called together the representatives of many faiths that he might choose between them. The followers of Confucius met the maulvies of Islam, and Roman Catholic fathers were confronted with a learned lama, head of the Sakya Monastery in southwestern Tibet.

The balance seems to have hovered between these last until a miracle turned the scale in favor of the Sa-kya abbot. He is said to have caused the emperor's cup to rise unlifted to his lips, a feat which the Romans were not able either to parallel or perform. The truth probably is that Lamaism was chosen as having most in common with the Shamanistic cults then prevailing over large areas in Mongolia and China. The emperor proclaimed it the state religion, and created the Sa-kya lama primate of the Lama church and tributary ruler of Tibet. This was in the year 1270.

Kublai Khan built many monasteries in Mongolia for the faith of his adoption, and also one at Peking. Thus in the fifth stage of its development Lamaism became a papacy, and the secular crown was placed on the spiritual head.

VI

We now come to Tson K'apa. Tson K'apa was the second reformer. He reformed the reformed sect of Atisa, which had sadly fallen away from its first ideals. Tson K'apa called out and gathered about him the more earnest among the monks, and set them to keep two hundred and thirty-five rigid rules. He lodged them in lamaseries, under the strictest discipline, and made them carry a begging-bowl, prayer-carpet, and other paraphernalia of Indian mendicant devotees. He also introduced a highly ritualistic service, which proved a great attraction. This abbot's influence marks the sixth epoch in the history of the Lama church. But who was he, and how did he acquire this influence? His career may be briefly described.

Tson K'apa was born near the Koko-Nor, at a place called Kumbum, now in the Chinese province of Kan-su. He is generally held to have borrowed many of his ideas from Roman Catholicism. His first teacher had a long nose; and this fact, being reported to Abbé Huc, convinced him that the teacher was a Roman Catholic priest. Mr. Rockhill, commenting on this, says: "The length of a nose is but a poor foundation for such an important theory; and, even if we accept noses as criterions, we shall find that those of Turkestan are quite as long as, if not longer than, our own." "But," he adds, "Marco Polo says there were Christians at Si-ning in the thirteenth century, and we know that in the fourteenth century Christianity flourished at Peking." By which I understand him to mean that he does not reject the supposition, while he ridicules the evidence on which it is based.

Tson K'apa went to Lhasa at seventeen years of age. In 1409 he built a monastery thirty miles east of the city, which he named Gahdan or Paradise; and at first his followers were called Gahlug-pa or "People of the Paradise Persuasion." This, being ill-sounding, was afterwards changed to Ge-lug-pa or "Disciples of the Virtuous Sect." [1]

The Ge-lug-pa soon eclipsed all other sects, and stole the papal crown from the Sa-kya lamas. It

[1] See Waddell's "Buddhism of Tibet," pp. 60, 61.

was first worn among them, in 1439, by Geden-dub, a nephew of Tson K'apa. Six years later this Grand Lama founded the monastery of Tashi-Lhunpo at Shigatze, which has often been described. About the same time Sera and De-pung were built, and these are the four chief lamaseries of the sect. It was Geden-dub who planted the seed of metempsychosis, or the reincarnation theory, which has led to such important results.

VII

Passing from the sixth to the last stage of Lamaistic development we must bridge over another period of two hundred years. This brings us to 1640, when a second Mongol conqueror, Gusri Khan, subdued Tibet. He came at the instance of a crafty and ambitious prelate, Nag-Wan-Lozan, who was head of the De-pung Monastery, and wished to grasp the supreme power over the general unrest and disturbance. Gusri Khan presented him with the sceptre of the conquered country, and he was afterwards confirmed in his kingly possession by the emperor of China, and was given the Mongol title of Dalai or "Ocean" Lama. The Tibetans themselves do not use this title; they prefer their own Gyal-wa Rim-po-ch'e or "Great Gem of Majesty."

Nagwan proclaimed himself to be an incarnation

of Avalokita, The Looking-Down One, the most popular of all Buddhist deities. And he raised the four Grand Lamas who had preceded him to the same exalted rank. Hitherto, the theory of reincarnation had contemplated only the continuance of a saint's life, the passing of his soul into another body at the moment of death. Now the idea was changed and glorified. The Grand Lama had not simply inherited the spirit of his predecessor, a man, but was actually the embodied presence of a divine being. "And the credulous populace felt their vanity flattered to have a deity incarnate as their king."

THE FIRST DALAI LAMA.

Nagwan removed his residence from De-pung to Lhasa, and built and named the great palace of Potala, from which all his successors have exercised their spiritual sway. He was the first Dalai Lama, but the fifth Grand Lama, or pope, of the Ge-lug-pa. He reigned for forty years, and even when he died, in 1680, his death was concealed for twelve years more by priests who ruled in his name.

His successor was dissolute, and was deposed and assassinated, which plunged the country into a sea of troubles ending in civil war. Then in 1722 the Chinese stepped in, and assumed that suzerainty which they have ever since claimed and maintained.

The Dalai Lama who was seen by Manning in 1811 was the ninth. The present one is the thirteenth, and was born in 1876, so that he is now twenty-five years of age. He is the only one for nearly a century who has been suffered to come of age and assume the reins of the temporal power. Recent events tend to show that more than the usual perils have beset his path. In a letter received from Yatung, under date of February 16, 1901, Miss Taylor reports as follows: "The Dalai Lama went on a pilgrimage during the summer, and visited his birthplace. On his return he had smallpox, and recovered, but his two brothers (who were with him) succumbed to the disease. Politically, there has been much unrest. The Tibetan chief, who was the Dalai Lama's tutor, and acted as king until he became of age, was accused of using sorcery to destroy the Lama's life. Three things were necessary for the purpose, two of them being a hair from the Dalai's head, and tartar from his teeth. He is said to have pulled out one of the Dalai's teeth when his holiness was eight years old. The three requisites having been secured, the chief wrapped them in paper and buried them in the grounds of Potala with many enchantments. These he repeated daily over the spot. But, just as the

AN AGED ABBOT.

MINSTREL MENDICANTS.

paper packet was about to take wings and depart (which would have meant the death of the Dalai), the tutor was caught and his evil deed discovered. The four members of the cabinet condemned him to death, but the Dalai would not consent to this sentence being carried out. He was therefore imprisoned, and has lately died."

Only second in repute to the Dalai Lama at Lhasa is the Tashi Lama, or abbot of the Tashi-Lhunpo Monastery. He also is worshipped as a divine being, the incarnation of Avalok's father, Amitabha; and the wily Nagwan seems to have suggested this convenient arrangement. It was evidently intended to quench possible rivalry, and to secure for the Tashi Lama a satisfying amount of homage, whilst the Dalai Lama would retain his supreme seat and power. The idea may have originated partly from feelings of gratitude, for it was a Tashi Lama who ordained Nagwan when he was a boy of seven. The third Tashi Lama was George Bogle's friend (1774), and the fourth was seen by Turner (1783). The fifth died in 1882, and the present one has held the position since 1888.

We have not done with the Grand Lamas yet. After the Dalai and the Tashi come four others. These are:

1. The Mongolia Grand Lama, at the monastery of Urgya-Kuren in Khalkas.

2. The Grand Lama of the Nin-ma-pa, or unreformed sect, at the Sakya Monastery.

3. The Dharma Raja of Bhutan, who belongs to the Dug-pa sect.

4. The celebrated abbess of the Yam-dok Lake.

All these are reckoned to be incarnations of some deity or other, but it would be wearisome to go into further detail.

We have seen how the image of Buddha, brought into a barbarous land as part of a bride's dower, began to shed a soft light on the surrounding coarseness, and presently found itself in the company of a host of others, very ugly, portentous, and grewsome, over whom it was expected to preside, and whose orgies it was called upon to sanction. Finally, a living idol was enthroned above it, and through all these vicissitudes the priests plied their unholy game for gold.

CHAPTER VIII

TIBETAN THEOLOGY

THE theology of the lamas is fearfully and wonderfully made. Like a handful of tangled thread, whichever end you pull at, the knotty middle only seems to get worse.

Major Waddell has written a most learned and laborious book on the subject, and has succeeded in making it marvellously interesting; but even he, with a properly appointed temple of his own to study, and friendly lamas ready to tell him all about it, seems to have felt himself more than once at sea in a mist. He calls the system "a chaotic crowd of gods, demons, and deified saints." And, after a careful perusal of his five hundred and ninety-eight pages, I subscribe to the truth of the statement.

Take a look at the literature. The Kah-gyur, or Tibetan Bible, consists of one hundred and eight volumes, of one thousand pages each, making one thousand and eighty-three separate books. Each of the volumes weighs about ten pounds, and forms a package twenty-six inches long by eight broad and eight deep. "This colossal code requires a dozen yaks for its transport, and the carved wooden blocks from which it is printed need for their storage rows of houses like a good-sized village." The contents are chiefly translations from Chinese and Sanskrit works. The original blocks are still being used after two hundred years, and almost every monastery has its complete printed edition.

In addition to this voluminous text there are two hundred and twenty-five volumes of commentaries, including works on general subjects, such as grammar, rhetoric, mechanics, alchemy, etc.

And we are not out of the wood yet. You may go on taking books from the shelves like things from a conjurer's hat, apparently *ad infinitum.* There is a large bundle, for instance, of "Revelations," which pretend to be the composition of Padma-sambhava, Tson K'apa, and others, obligingly hidden away by them in caves and corners of the land to give prophetic sanction to special sects and sites. They were of course "discovered" as they happened to be wanted from time to time.

BELL AND IMAGE FOUNDRY.

Add to these a heap of legendary stories and one

book containing no less than one hundred thousand songs, partly in praise of Tara, the consort of Avalokita, and goddess of mercy, partly in the nature of directions for making "magic circles."

Such is the muddle into which the riotous imagination of Hindoostan, unchilled by the snows and frosts of Tibet, has led the Lama scribes. Yet the people have the utmost reverence for their sacred books and pay them divine honors. The Kah-gyur is worshipped with lamps and incense, even little fragments of it being carefully treasured. The paper on which it is printed is made from the bark of a tree, and the printing is of the roughest description; but a great price is willingly paid for complete impressions. The Peking edition is said to have sold for £600, and a tribe of Mongols bought their copy for seven thousand oxen.

You do not know a man till you know his mind. But the Tibetan mind is like the Tibetan lake, which reflects, so clear is the air, every bird that poises for a moment above it, and every shaggy beast that stands at its edge, framed by the black rocks around. Buddhism came up and peeped into the lake, and Buddhism in gorgeous tints is mirrored there forevermore. Not primitive Buddhism, which was merely a proclamation of simple precepts, but the Buddhism of a thousand years after its founder's death; including such opposites as Yoga, or ecstatic union with the All-Spirit by means of "a self-hypnotizing process which could be learned by rules;" and Tantrism, or the coarse worship of the energy of nature through the goddess Kali and other forms; not to mention a perfect labyrinth of laws and ceremonials between. All this profusion of thought and practice was enshrined in the yellow books that Buddhism carried on its back over the Himalayas. And these were dumped down into the midst of a demons' land already alive with legends and wet with the blood of sacrifices; a land of mythical white lions roaring in storms, and wild, hairy men dwelling amidst the eternal snows, and fierce dragons introduced from China.

Lamaism swallowed the whole,—a most indigestible mass. Still there are some ideas which seem to have gained a certain coherence and permanence. For instance, Sakya Muni[1] is reckoned to be only one of a series of "human Buddhas" who are called "those who have gone before." These look on to another yet to come, whose name is Jam-pa (Sanskrit, Maitreya) "The Loving One." There is an image of Jampa at Lhasa, which rises through a three-storied building, up which the pilgrims go spirally, first travelling round the feet, then the trunk, and finally the jewelled head. The image is made of clay coated with gold.

[1] The historical Buddha.

The lotus has been adopted from India as the favorite emblem of the supernatural. "It seems to spring from the body of the waters without contact with the sordid earth, and, no matter how muddy the water may be, the lotus preserves its own purity undefiled."[1] Like the growth of this flower out of darkness and mystery into form and beauty is the conception of the birth and blooming of Buddhas. Underlying all, invisible and eternal, is the Adi Buddha. By meditation (dhyan) he has evolved five celestial creations which, like the flat leaves, lie still and impassive on the waters. These are Dhyani Buddhas, the intermediate but inactive sources of the five elements and the five senses. Then come the Bodhisats, the five celestial and active agents of the silent Dhyanis. These communicate with men by means of human reflexes, or doubles, and ever seek the well-being of the world.

Human Buddhas, that is, saints who have attained nirvana, or absorption in the All-Spirit, sometimes elect, from love of their fellows, to relinquish that reward of merit, and become Bodhisats, that they may return to earth, and teach men the perfect way.

The most popular of the Bodhisats are,—

1. Manjusri, the "sweet-voiced" god of wisdom. In his right hand is the bright sword of knowledge

[1] "Lamaism," p. 388.

ready "to cut all knotty points," and in his left are the scriptures resting on a lotus.

2. Vagrapani, "wielder of the thunderbolt." He is a fierce fiend, painted either black or blue, with a dorje in his hand.

3. Avalokita, the "one who has looked, or looks, down." His Tibetan name is Chenraisi. He is pictured seated on a lotus, like his consort Tara, and has sometimes eleven faces, but always a multitude of eyes. The hands are outstretched in blessing, and there are pitying eyes placed in the palms. This is the "jewel in the lotus" of the lamas' mystic formula, "*Om Mani Padme Hum*," "O jewel in the lotus, O."

The heaven of the Tibetans, like that of the Chinese and Japanese, is Sukhavati, the "Happy Land," the golden "Gates of the West," whither the suns hasten and disappear in a glorious glow. It is presided over by Amitabha, the father of Avalokita, and is the prize given to those who worship his son.

The "wheel of life," not wholly a Buddhist conception, occupies a large space in Tibetan thought. It is a pointed disc divided into six compartments. The circle symbolizes endless existence, and the six compartments show the six regions of rebirth. The wheel is clutched by a monster to signify the hideousness of clinging to life. At the centre are the

THE WHEEL OF LIFE.

three images of desire,—a bird, a serpent, and a pig; and round the tire are painted pictures representing the twelve links in the chain of causality.

The six regions of rebirth include the animal world, a world of tantalized ghosts, and hot and cold hells. But this is a grewsome subject; let us drop it. Suffice it to say, as Gilmour has put it, "there is one thing worth remarking; that is, the fitness of the punishment to the sin. Take one example. A man has lived and died a glutton. The consequence is that he is punished by hunger. He is born again with a body perhaps as large as a a mountain and a stomach capacious as a cavern; food is within his reach, and he is as hungry as all the wolves in Siberia; he would eat, but his mouth is as small as a needle's eye, and his throat is as narrow as a hair. Gluttony was his sin, and hunger is his punishment. It is the same all through; a man's punishment springs directly from his sin."

The figure of Buddha is always pictured outside the wheel, to show that he has escaped from its giddy toils.

CHAPTER IX

MONK AND MONASTERY

YOU might travel for a year in Tibet, and hear very little of the meaning of the sacred books, but you could not possibly miss meeting the monks,—they are as thick on the ground as mushrooms,—or fail to be struck by the number and strength of the castellated monasteries scattered up and down the land. The mind of the lama is a chamber of mystery, fantastically adorned, and tenanted by ghosts; but the man himself is real enough, and a picturesque figure to boot. We have had enough of metaphysics and "the stuff that dreams are made of"; let us get into the open air. This is solid earth we are treading, and these are substantial superstructures of stone.

You can tell a monk by his dress. The garments of "sad saffron," which Buddha prescribed, survive in a dirty petticoat of dingy red, fastened by a girdle to match. Above this is worn the "patched robe," an emblem of poverty, leaving the right arm bare. From the girdle depends a chatelaine of sacred implements, including a leathern bottle, a pen-case, purse, etc. The boots are of stiff red felt, with yak-hair soles, and come half-way up to the knees.

But the most distinctive feature is the cap or cowl. Petticoat and robe mark the genus monk; the hat indicates the species, the sect.

A LAMA'S HAT.

ANYBODY'S HAT.

There is quite a bewildering variety of shapes and sizes, and each is symbolical of something; but the main patterns are three, and their colors are black, red, and yellow.

The black hat is a madcap piece of head-gear, round and fly-away in shape, and adorned with a collection of feathers and fancies. It is the hat of the Bon-pa, the sect of the aboriginal devil-dancers; and certainly it suits them.

The red hat is shaped like a mitre, with turned-up flaps, the conventional form of the lotus. It belongs to the Nin-ma-pa, the first or unreformed sect, the "Auld Lichts" of Lamaism.

The yellow hat is also like a mitre; only it runs up to a sharp point and trails down on each side in long flaps. This modification was made by Tson

K'apa, who founded the Ge-lug-pa, or "Reformed Virtuous Order Sect"; and this has ever since been the "state church" in Tibet.

These distinctive colors, especially the red and the yellow, are carried through all the details of life. The red hats live in houses with red stripes, and use red rosaries, and love the red lotus, while the yellow hats rival them with their own special tint.

The rosary is in every one's hand. Dr. Waddell thinks this fact has not received sufficient attention. The reason probably is that the familiarity of the object to Western travellers made it less conspicuous than the curious "prayer-cylinder," in shape not unlike a baby's rattle, which is equally used. Telling the beads is called by the Tibetans "purring like a cat," and it is not a bad metaphor, as a low mumbling noise is kept up all the time. So assiduously is the habit practised that sometimes the bulbous beads are worn down to the thinness of little tubes.

Rosaries are of many kinds. The yellow beads are made from a tree in central China. The rough brown seeds used by the red-caps fall from trees on the outer Himalayas. Each special deity has its favorite kind. Avalokita is worshipped with a rosary made of white discs of the conch-shell. The demons prefer discs cut from the human skull.

Other kinds are made of glass, crystal, snake spines, a hard substance found in the brain of the elephant, red sandal-wood, and nuts.

The lamaseries are called Gompas (Gon-pa, a solitary people), and are very numerous. There are said to be three thousand of them in Tibet. They are built of sun-dried bricks, or stone, timber being

LAMASERY NEAR REH-HO, MANCHURIA.

very scarce. As a rule, they stand in isolated positions, and often on almost inaccessible heights. "Some of them are quite cut off from the outer world, and even at favorable times can only be reached by dangerous paths." Some are so large that they resemble towns, having long streets of cells, two or three stories high, with enclosed courts. In these the chief central building is both an assembly-hall and a temple. Most have flat roofs, surmounted by huge prayer cylinders made of yak-hair cloth, and strings of rags and flags.

A monastery must be built on consecrated ground, with its back to the mountain. It must face the east, with, if possible, a lake gleaming in the prospect.

"Back to the hill rock,
Front to the tarn."

The approach to a monastery is always through lines of chortens, flag-poles, and scraggy trees. The chorten (receptacle for offerings) is a masonry monument erected in memory of some lama saint, or as a depository for relics. It is a copy of the "stupa" of the Indian Buddhists. The original form was a massive dome[1] (womb), on an elaborate plinth, with a square capital crowned by an umbrella, the symbol of royalty. Later developments added a blunt spire of thirteen bands, typical of the thirteen heavens. On the top might be a bell, a lotus, a crescent moon, or a globular sun. The Tibetans keep the general characteristics, but have inverted the dome. Ashes of lamas, sacred books, and other relics are placed in a niche left for the purpose.

The poles and flags seem to be of mixed descent, partly Indian and partly Chinese. Every schoolboy has heard of the famous Edicts of Asoka.[2] Asoka was the Constantine of Buddhism, and he inaugurated the practice of erecting "pillars" inscribed

[1] See picture of the oldest extant—at Sarnath, Benares.

[2] Pronounced Awshōk.

1. The Stupa at Sarnath, near Benares.
2. The Lamas' Blackboard.
3, 4. The Lion Pillar at Lauriya, erected by Asoka.
5. A Chorten.

with pious wishes and extracts from "the law," that these might be displayed aloft. Six of the pillars set up by him in India are still standing, and they were planted in the ground more than twenty centuries ago (B. C. 253–251). The one that is best preserved, and alone retains its original capital, is the Lion Pillar at Lauriya in the district of Champarun. Its height is thirty-nine feet, six inches. Under the capital is the usual garland of Brahmani geese. But the pillars of Asoka are stone; what have they to do with the wooden poles of the Tibetan flags? The transition was effected in Burmah. The Buddhist temples in Burmah are provided with tall masts and streaming banners. Each mast has a Brahmani goose carved upon it, and the streamers (light wicker frames pasted over with paper) are often inscribed with pious sentences in imitation of Asoka's example. Timber is cheap and stone dear in Burmah. Few, like the emperor, could raise pillars of stone, but any man might put up little posts of wood. The Tibetans, like the Burmese, adopted the wooden pole, but their flags have usually a lion in one of the upper corners and a bird below. These are relics of the lion capital and the garland of geese.

But the Tibetan flags have generally, in addition, a dragon-headed horse in the middle, and this is undoubtedly a representation of one of the four great mythical animals of China, the Horse Dragon, the symbol of grandeur.[1]

SOME OF THE CHIEF MONASTERIES

1. The most powerful and populous of all the lamaseries is that at De-pung (Rice-Heap), three miles west of Lhasa. It clusters round the great temple, which is resplendent with a golden roof. Seven thousand monks are said to be in residence. The body of the fourth Grand Lama is preserved in a chorten near.

2. The second monastery of importance is that of Serra, one and a half miles north of Lhasa. "Serra" means "Hail," and the hail is to destroy the rice. This monastery contains five thousand five hundred monks, and some hideous-headed images. Perched above it on almost inaccessible ledges of rock are solitary cells to which the more ascetic sometimes retire. All the walls of its three large temples are overlaid with gold. Serra is specially famous as the place where the original dorje[2] or ecclesiastical sceptre is preserved. It flew through the air from India, and is the model for all others. Once a year it is carried to Lhasa to be worshipped. The Dalai Lama puts it reverently to his head; so does the Chinese amban; so do all the

[1] See "Buddhism in Tibet," pp. 408–413.

[2] This word gives its name to Darjiling, *rdorje* and *glin*, a place.

great officials in turn, and their example is followed by thousands of others.

3. Third in rank is the monastery of Tashi Lhunpo (heap of glory). It is situated a mile from Shigatze, near the south bank of the Tsanpo. It is quite a town. Five gates pierce the wall. On the east gate is a notice prohibiting the smoking of tobacco. Four thousand monks live within the walls. The temple has a roof supported by a hundred pillars. It can accommodate an audience of two thousand seated on mats on the floor. The most interesting building at Tashi Lhunpo is that called the Kiku Tamsa. It is nine stories high, and tapers upward like a wedge or like the broad blade of a hatchet. It is the lamas' larder, being filled with dried carcasses of sheep, yak, and goat, for the monastic table. But it is also a gigantic blackboard or picture screen, and this purpose determined its peculiar shape.

A large enclosure fronts the building, and twice a year, in June and November, immense crowds gather to gaze on the silken pictures of Buddhist deities which are hung over it for exhibition. These pictures are a hundred feet long. The chief favorite is Jampa, the "Loving One," the Buddha that is to be. Pilgrims come from long distances to see this picture, and press forward to kiss its silken fringe. It is impossible not to think of Him whose love constrains every Christian heart, and will yet draw all men unto him. He alone, and no other, is the unknown Friend of these simple Tibetans; and we cannot doubt that he will heal their sorrows and visit their souls, as he healed the woman in the Gospels when she came behind and "touched the hem of his garment."

4. Another monastery of renown is that of Sakya (Tawny Soil). It is fifty miles north of Everest, and said to be the largest single building in Tibet. It is famous for its great library, the books of which are of extraordinary size and the lettering embossed in gold and silver.

5. The Sam-ding Lamasery, in the curious Yamdok (or Scorpion) Lake,[1] contains both monks and nuns, and is presided over by a woman. She is now (1901) forty-five years of age, and was seen by Baboo Sarat Chandra Das on his journey to Lhasa. The monastery stands on a barren rock three hundred feet high, facing the island between the claws. A long flight of stone steps, guarded by a wall, leads up to the gates. "In a private, strongly barred chamber, to which no one may be admitted,

[1] This lake is one hundred and twenty miles in circumference and thirteen thousand eight hundred feet above the level of the sea. Its claws embrace a peninsula which rises to a height above sixteen thousand feet and is grass-grown to the summit, embosoming another lake which is twenty-four miles round and five hundred feet above the level of the first. See article "Tibet," in Encyclopædia Britannica.

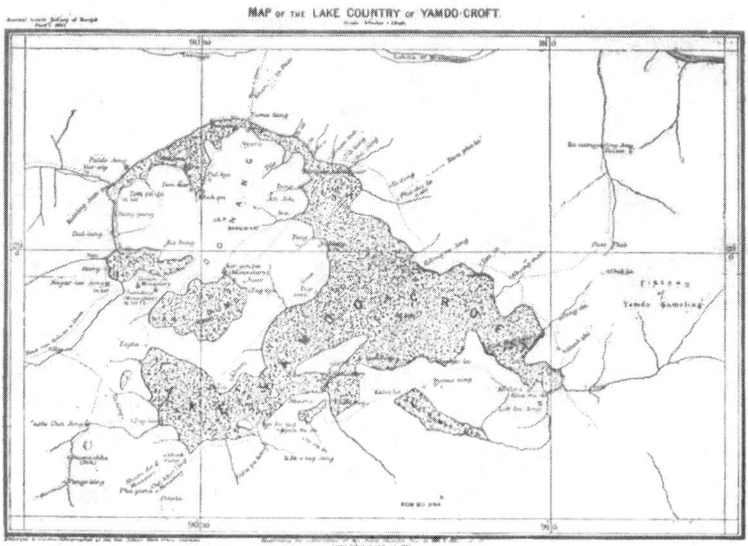

THE CURIOUS "SCORPION LAKE."

BRICK TEA.

are laid the mortal remains of all the former incarnations of the goddess. Here, in this melancholy apartment, will be one day placed the body of the present lady abbess, after embalmment. To the grim charnel-house it is considered the imperative duty of each incarnate abbess to repair once while living, to gaze her fill on her predecessors, and to make formal obeisance to their mouldering forms. She *must* enter once, but only once, during her lifetime."[1] This lady is known all over Tibet as the Diamond Sow, and you are not to laugh at this; it is a title of honor. Two centuries ago the monastery was attacked by a Mongol chieftain, and its first abbess miraculously defended its treasure. The warrior battered in the gates, but was astonished to find only a few pigs and sows wandering about the yard. He could hardly plunder a place guarded simply by hogs. Suddenly they were all transformed into venerable-looking monks and nuns, and his heart was won.

It is reported that the present lady never suffers herself to sleep in a recumbent position. She dozes in a chair all day, and at night sits up through the long hours wrapped in meditation. Occasionally she pays a visit to Lhasa, and is received with the greatest veneration.

6. The monastery at Peking is called "Ever-

[1] "Lamaism," p. 276.

lasting Peace." It houses a thousand monks, mostly Mongolians. In the chief temple there is a wooden image of Buddha seventy feet high. The toe measures twenty-one inches. The idol holds an enormous lotus in each hand, and wears a jewel on his breast. Galleries go round him, and two magnificent bronze lions stand by his side. The building is richly draped with silk screens and Tibetan carpets.

7. The Kumbum Monastery was erected in memory of Tson K'apa, at his birthplace near the Koko-Nor. The famous white sandal-tree is said to have sprung up miraculously at his birth, and to bear an image, or some sacred writing, in the fibre of each one of its hundred thousand leaves. M. Huc saw it, and declared there was no deception; "the characters all appeared to us portions of the leaf itself, equally with its veins and nerves; the position was not the same in all, and the younger leaves represented them only in a partial state of formation. . . . The perspiration absolutely trickled down our faces under the influence of the sensations which this most amazing spectacle created."[1] Other travellers have found it a little difficult to verify this description, and the reason assigned is that "only firm believers can now trace anything on the leaves."

[1] Huc, ii., p. 53.

8. The monastery of the Mongolian Grand Lama at Urgya is forty days' journey west of Peking. It has twenty-eight colleges and fourteen thousand monks. The broad plain which stretches away from its base is covered with tents for the use of pilgrims.

9. The He-mi or Himis monastery, in Ladakh, is eighteen miles from Leh. A great festival is celebrated there annually in the summer, on St. Padma's day. This Himis fair forms the chief attraction to many tourists in Kashmir. Masquerades last from morning till night. The monks array themselves in terrible or grotesque disguises, and go through droll antics, acting a series of dramas, which are intended to impress the minds of the laity with the importance of lama ministrations—their helplessness in the clutch of devils without a priest to defend and deliver them.

WORSHIP AND TRAINING OF THE MONKS

The central portion of every monastery is the temple, and, similarly, even private houses have a separate room, or at least an altar, for the daily worship.

The temple interiors are richly colored, "the walls being covered with frescos and the beams painted red, picked out with lotus rosettes and other emblems." The "wheel of life" is generally pictured in the vestibule. Above the altar are the "Three Precious Ones"; namely, Buddha, The Law, and The Church. This is the Buddhist Trinity. Symbols of the "Three" must always be present when worship is going on, wherever that may be. An image will stand for Buddha, a book for the law, and a chorten (in miniature) for the church.

Every day, in every temple of Lamaism, a model of the universe is offered to Buddha. It is built up of rice and dough, with much ceremony and muttering of mantras, at the close of which it is presented with the following prayer: "Let all animals enjoy happiness! Let us be delivered from this delusive world!"

The temple seats are arranged in a definite order, the monks and novices being placed on each side of the nave, seated on long, low cushions. At the further end of the right-hand cushion is the abbot's throne, with a seat for his assistant below. Opposite these are seats for the manager of the establishment and his assistant,—who are also the chief choristers. Near the door is a table on which tea and soup are placed to be passed round in the intervals of worship. In the porch are the "prayer-barrels," huge as the space will allow, and opposite the door is the altar. The altar should have at least two tiers. On the lower ledge are the offerings of water, rice, flowers, and lamps. On the higher are the following: a chorten, one or more sacred books, a dorje, a holy-water vase, a metal mirror, cymbals, a conch-shell trumpet, a pair of long telescopic copper horns, a pair of human thigh-bone trumpets,[1] and three drums. The big drum is sometimes suspended in a frame, sometimes pierced by a pole. One of the small ones is shaped like a double egg-cup, and beaten by knobs attached to it with thongs. The other is made of a human skull.

LAMA'S TRUMPET (often made of human thigh-bone).

The course of training for a lama is long and severe. He is sent to school to the monastery at the age of eight. He is medically examined, his horoscope is tested, and if all is satisfactory a tutor is assigned him, whose menial slave he must thenceforth be. He is taught the alphabet, and commits to memory some golden maxims and small manuals of duty. His relatives call to see him once a month. This goes on for two or three years, during which he is called a probationer (da-pa). Then his tutor introduces him to the brotherhood, an agreement is made and sealed by an impression of the thumb, his name is registered, a scarf is presented with silver coins, his head is shaved, he solemnly takes

[1] The bones of criminals or those who have died by violence are preferred. The maker has to eat a portion of the skin to make the blast effectual.

the vows and receives a religious name. Then at his own or his parents' expense all the monks have to be entertained at tea. He is now a novitiate (ge-tsul). For twelve years more he must study and wait before he can become a ge-lon or fully ordained monk. And the curriculum comprises books of magic, the legendary histories of lama saints, and many of the books of Buddhism. There are frequent examinations, and still more frequent public disputations, at which, before an audience of sometimes two thousand "brothers" the lama elect exercises his powers.

No doubt many of them, for the most part, scamp their work; but, all the same, there would seem to be some truth in the Tibetan proverb,

> "He who eats lamas' food
> Wants iron jaws."

CHAPTER X

IN THE HOMES OF THE PEOPLE

THE Tibetans are a laughter-loving people, but unspeakably dirty. They do not wash, their garments are "a zoölogical preserve," and their homes are as savory as themselves.[1] But they have some excuse. The climate is such that your very hair freezes on your face, and a man has to be a walking mattress, rolled in a mackintosh bag, to keep warm at all.

The women paint their cheeks with a thick layer of dirty-brown pigment erroneously supposed by Europeans in India to be made of pigs' blood. The origin of the custom is not certainly known. Some suppose it to have been ordered by a zealous lama, with a view to reducing the attractions of the sex and so lessening their influence over the

[1] Mr. Rockhill, who knew them well, and moved familiarly amongst them on all occasions, and in their own country, gives us a glimpse of what it means: "To-day has been employed receiving dirty men and women, showing and explaining to them the various foreign things I carry with me, asking occasionally a question and endeavoring to elicit information without exciting suspicion. It is horribly tedious, and a sad strain on one's patience, but a part of my work."—"Diary."

minds of his monks. There can be no question about the effect of the practice; anything more disgusting than these bloated-looking faces it would be difficult to imagine. But the real reason was probably much simpler—to keep out the cold. The men smear themselves with butter.

If there is no cleanliness, neither is there any comfort. The houses are rough two-storied structures of rubble stone or sun-dried bricks (sometimes even of yak dung), with flat roofs. Rude steps lead up to the top from outside, and the roof itself is like a London back yard on washing-day, with its strings of ragged cloth fluttering in the breeze. These are the well-known "prayer-flags." The ground floor is occupied by cattle, and the people use the rooms above. There is no chimney, merely a hole in the roof to admit the light and give egress to the smoke.

Whole tribes of the inhabitants are nomads, dwelling in tents. Some of these are really huts covered with felt. Others are "black tents" of yak-hair sacking, more like the coarse meshes of a fishing-net than anything else. They are hexagonal in form, and "bear no slight resemblance to a great spider standing motionless on its long, lanky legs, but so that its stomach is resting on the ground. They are very cold, and a strong wind knocks them down without the least difficulty."[1]

[1] Huc, ii., pp. 79, 80.

INTERIOR OF HUT ON THE BORDER, SHOWING THE K'ANG.

RAJAH'S PALACE AT TUMLUNG.

On the borders of China Tibetan huts have a raised mud platform in the centre, called the ka'ang. It is used as a cooking-range and also as a warming-stove and a bed. You sit or recline upon it till one part of your body is warm, and then roll gently over to distribute the heat.

There is no furniture in the houses; nothing but a few boxes, pots and pans, saddle gear, dried meat, and skins containing stores.

But there is a house god, and he is a very uncomfortable sort of guest. Like the kitchen god of China he has the head of a pig. And he is extremely restless. He wanders from corner to corner of the house, and is a constant source of anxiety and distress. While he is standing in the corner, of course it cannot be swept; while he is sitting on a box or a stool, it would be sacrilege to sit upon him. His movements are all set down in the calendar, but, as he is at all times invisible, and you are apt to forget where his presence ought to be on a particular date, it is exceedingly awkward. Moreover, he is prone to be vindictive if you make a mistake. But he is a very knowing god; his place is always at the fire in the coldest season, and outside the door in summer.

The Tibetans whitewash their houses occasionally, but not inside. The method was observed by Captain Wellby during his stay at Kumbum. They mix the wash, ascend the roof, and pour it down over the walls.

The character of the common people is mild and sometimes jovial. Murder is scarcely known except among the wilder tribes. Buddhism has given them a great reverence for human life. But they are notorious thieves and facile perverters of the truth. Contact with the wily Chinaman has not improved them in this respect. Through it all they are kind-hearted, hospitable, and faithful friends.

Their family life is peculiar. One woman has generally several husbands, but the husbands are always brothers. The wife is their common property, but it seldom happens that more than one of them is at home at a time. The others are absent with the cattle or for purposes of trade. A belle is purchased from her parents, and sometimes costs thirty yaks. The Tibetans like and defend this custom of fraternal polyandry. They regard it as economical, and as tending to keep the family together and to build up the estate. Moreover, it releases a certain number of the males for necessary pastoral work away from home, and for the long journeys they have sometimes to take. It would be difficult to find an asylum for the wife if she was not also the wife of the wanderer's brother. The women especially appreciate the arrangement. With only one husband, they would become widows at his death; having many, they are never widows.

As for the absent trader, he usually contracts a temporary marriage with some one else. A period is fixed; it may be merely a month, or it may extend to one or two years, and the marriage is binding till the period expires. There is very little polygamy, however, in the true sense, though some of the wealthy practise it in the southern parts, influenced by the Indian habit.

Marriage amongst the common people is a very loose institution. The pair generally live together for a time, to see whether they suit each other, before the contract is made. If they do, a day is appointed, neighbors come in and adorn them with the silken scarf, and a feast crowns the ceremony. But, after all, these unions are not of a binding nature. The bride forsakes her husband for a richer, and the bridegroom discards his wife when she has ceased to please.

The Tibetan woman has been called "a drudge and a queen." She does all the hard work, has property of her own, and practically rules the roost.

Her dress on gala occasions is gorgeous. You should see her hair! In the wilder parts of the country it resembles a tousled mop, but elsewhere, especially in the neighborhood of Lhasa, it is plaited into a hundred strings and spread out flat over a great train of embroidered cloth, which gradually widens out and falls down the back, richly bestudded with turquoise and coral set in massive brooches or bands of silver. She also wears heavy earrings of the same kind, and a jewelled cloth down the forehead, not unlike the silver ornaments with which a rajah adorns his elephant. And her hands are heavy with silver rings. The lavish amount of precious stones and metals displayed on the persons of the Tibetan women, even those who are comparatively poor, suggests the conclusion that the country is a mine of minerals and would yield immense quantities of silver and gold. Captain Bower says: "Women dressed in dirty sheepskins often wear several hundred rupees' worth of silver ornaments, while a gold bead here and there is not uncommon. And a man may often be seen drinking tea out of an extremely inferior porcelain cup, with a silver saucer, cover, and spoon." "The men," says Mr. Rockhill,[1] "wear nearly as much jewelry as the women, ornamenting with silver their sword-hilts and scabbards, their saddles, guns, tinder-boxes, and wooden bowls, besides wearing earrings, rings, and charm-boxes made of that metal and set with coral and turquoise beads."

The Tibetans are fond of children, but, unlike

[1] See the excellent series of articles published by the famous traveller in *The Century Magazine*, 1890–91.

TYPICAL TIBETANS.

the Chinese, are rather callous in their treatment of the old. There is of course less of child-life than in other lands. But it is none the less prattling and playful. The boys belong to the father and the girls to the mother. The baby at birth is rubbed over with butter and oil. On the fifteenth day it can be bathed, but the head must be carefully excluded from the process, or bad luck will overtake the parents.

Two days after birth, in the case of a girl, and three days in the case of a boy, all the neighbors and friends come to rejoice with the house. They bring chang,[1] an intoxicating drink, and scarfs of blessing, one of which is placed round the neck of the child, and one each is given to the parents. Then they settle down to drinking, dancing, and singing, prolonging the revel far into the night, till all are drunk. The mother, if she is wise, tastes a little and goes off to sleep.

As the child grows, it is taught to blow the fire,[2] fetch water, stir the food in the pot, collect fuel, and do other little things about the house. When

[1] Chang is a kind of beer. Mr. F. B. Shawe, late of Leh, says that "it is the main cause of poverty in Ladakh." In no case is drunkenness a disgrace. See the interesting series of articles entitled "Nine Centuries of Buddhism," in *The Missionary Review of the World*, 1896.

[2] This is done by means of a goatskin sewed up on one side and fitted into an iron nozzle,—a very effective but clumsy bellows.

old enough, it is sent to look after the cattle. Boys who are destined for the cloisters go off to school. They have rather a rough time of it there, being beaten across the chest with a broad leather strap for every failure to remember the lesson and every defect in writing. Their slate is a wooden tablet painted black. It is smeared over with fat and sprinkled with powdered chalk. The writing is done with a wooden pen which removes the chalk and reveals the black. If a boy disgraces himself by continual laziness, or incompetence, his tutor is publicly caned. What do you think of that?

The theory of transmigration, or an endless round of re-births, colors all the life of the people. It is celebrated in song and story; accounts for special friendships, even between men and animals; and condones crime. It provides the lamas with a terrible engine of torture and oppression. They have dice-boards for divination, and load their dice. The squares on the board are painted to represent the regions of re-birth, and the numbers on the dice correspond. A number turns up which augurs a horrible fate, and the superstitious victim is fleeced to secure the counteracting aid of the priest.

Charms and amulets are worn by everybody. They generally contain some scrap of sacred writing which is folded in a cloth packet, tied with colored thread, or in a metal case, along with relics of holy men, such as threads of the cast-off clothing of saints or idols, and peacock feathers, etc. For domestic broils the talisman consists of a mystic monogram wrapped in a charm paper and tied with a twisted thread made of the hairs of a dog, a goat, and a sheep. The whole is enclosed in the skin of a mouse. As these are all creatures about the house, the idea is said to be the union of domestic elements. As a preventive against the attacks of ferocious watch-dogs, all travellers carry a charm which contains the picture of a dog fettered and muzzled and chained to a dorje. Drawings of horses, on paper, are sometimes sent "on the wings of the wind" to assist belated travellers or those caught in a storm.

Sorcery is continually resorted to. A state sorcerer goes to Lhasa annually, in great pomp, and, Zadkiel-like, prophesies the events of the year. He calls on the Dalai Lama, but on no one else. All lesser officials have to go to him. His help is considered indispensable in guiding the ship of state. Practically he sets the course. His charge for a consultation may be anything from ten to ten thousand tankas.[1] The applicant must have his request presented in writing. When these have accumulated in sufficient numbers, a curtain is drawn aside, and the oracle is disclosed in a wildly ecstatic

[1] A tanka is worth about sixpence.

state. He throws rice at the applicants, and finally falls down in convulsions, and replies to the questions addressed. A man may ask, "How shall I get rain on my farm?" And the answer is sure to be something like this: "Plant prayer-flags."

When sickness comes into a Tibetan house, the greatest care is taken to prevent the patient from sleeping, especially in the daytime, as that is considered fatal. Lamas are engaged to ward off the evil spirits, and they keep up a dreadful noise, day and night, clashing their cymbals and beating their drums. Diseases are supposed to be cured by purchasing a charm and swallowing the paper on which it is written, or washing off the reflection of the writing in a mirror and drinking the water. Mr. Shawe tells a story of a sick man who, having swallowed several leaves of Buddhist books without finding relief, ate a few pages of the Bible. He was bitterly disappointed to find that the new religion eased him as little as the old.

The lamas use their power to the utmost in the pursuit of gain. To quote Mr. Shawe again: "As soon as a man cannot pay, or refuses to pay, the lamas blast him by their curse. . . . He sees himself delivered helpless into the hands of evil powers. His crops will fail; his cattle will die; he himself and his family will be attacked by loathsome diseases. The lamas are neither loved nor respected. Their power is due to fear and fear alone."[1]

The administration of justice is barbarous. Only lamas may sit on the bench. The culprit has his choice. He may either pay the fine or be maimed. The grossest criminal can purchase immunity from punishment. The commonest offence is stealing. No Tibetan will leave you alone in his room. He would not trust his own brother. Pilfering is a fine art amongst them. Half the beggars of Lhasa are said to go about minus a hand, foot, or eye,—the result of a conviction in the courts. Thieves are sometimes thrashed with thorns and sent naked into the mountains. Prisoners are cruelly tortured. Capital punishment is inflicted by drowning, thus avoiding the taking of life by bloodshedding, of which their Buddhist ideas have given them a horror.

The people run after shows, processions, and performances of all sorts, and are very fond of a mournful kind of music. This instinct gives the lamas another chance, which they do not fail to improve. But their richest harvest is reaped through death.

When a Tibetan dies, the body is not disturbed till a lama comes and extracts the soul. Any movement of the corpse might eject it, and then it would float upward like the flying ants of India, and per-

[1] *The Missionary Review of the World*, July, 1896.

haps be seized by demons as they are seized by the birds. A white cloth covers the face of the dead. When the lama arrives, he seats himself at the head of the body amidst a solemn silence. All the doors and windows are carefully closed. Then he chants directions for the soul's journey to Sukhavat, and finally with his forefinger and thumb he seizes a few hairs from the crown and plucks them out. This is supposed to perforate the skull and permit the spirit to escape.

Meanwhile lama astrologers are engaged in preparing the death horoscope, which fixes the time and method of disposal, and the special sort of worship to be made. Then the body is bound tightly with cords, in a sitting posture, and fastened to a corner of the room. Notice of the funeral is sent to the relatives. Feasting begins and lasts for some days, a portion of each dish being offered to the dead. All day and night the lamas chant a book, dividing the leaves amongst them, and doing it in relays of three or four, who gabble off their parts simultaneously, the merit consisting solely in the quantity got through. They are paid, like the lawyers, at so much a page.

Often these pretenders declare that the poor fellow has gone to hell, and hence a much more costly service must be paid for to get him out. When this is over, they affirm, perhaps, that it has not been fully efficacious; the spirit is partly out, but still partly in, and the whole service must be gone over again and doubly paid for.

On the day fixed for the funeral there is another feast, and then the procession starts. A scarf is presented, and one end of it fastened to the body. Some relative takes the bundle on his back, and the lama leads the way, towing it along by the scarf, and waggling his hand-drum while he blows the thigh-bone trumpet. Every now and then he looks back to beckon the departed spirit on with the body. If the dead be a lama, there is no need for this; the spirits of the lamas know their way by instinct.

The procession climbs to the top of a hill, and there the body is buried, cremated, or cut up and given to the eagles. These swoop down to take the pieces as they are offered. There is no indignity attaching to this custom. It is considered an honor to have living burial in the bodies of the birds. The real reason for the practice is doubtless the difficulty of burial in the ordinary way when the ground is hard and frozen. Cremation is too expensive in a timberless land, and there remains only the method of exposure. The body is sometimes given to the fishes, as at the Yam-dok Lake, and more often handed to the dogs. Some lamaseries keep dogs for the purpose.

These are but a few of the rites and ceremonies

prescribed and indulged in, at the expense of the relatives, when a death occurs. The ashes of lamas, after cremation, or the ashes of the paper effigy, if the body was devoured, are made into a paste with clay, and pressed into medallions, the possession of which is greatly prized.

The Tibetans make good potters, moulders of images, and workers in metal and stone. As early as three centuries ago one of themselves engineered eight iron-chain suspension bridges over the Tsanpo. Several of these stand to-day. This man was a genius and is canonized as a saint. But there is no question that a large amount of similar talent lies latent in the country for want of proper appreciation and patronage. The makers of gold plates for covering the roofs of temples are in great demand. The bell-foundries and large image-workshops have been described by Huc. The land is full of idols. Every rock is a pedestal, every house a shrine.

Pictures, too, abound. The artists are almost exclusively lamas. Pictures are painted on canvas or cotton smeared with lime and flour. The outline is drawn by means of a stencil plate perforated by holes, not unlike the perforated cards given to children of the kindergarten; and over this charcoal dust is sifted. The colors are loud and harsh. They are put on with hot, thin glue. This makes the pictures perishable in damp weather. They are mounted on rollers, like Japanese screens, and the artist draws a little portrait of himself in the corner, in an attitude of adoration.

The most curious of all lamaistic works of art are the famous bas-reliefs in tinted butter, to be seen at Kumbum. Butter is a favorite material for plastic work all over the country, but here it reaches its greatest glory. Mr. Rockhill writes:[1] "The bas-reliefs were about thirty feet long and ten feet high, supported by a frame-work and lighted up by rows of little brass bowls filled with butter in which burned cotton wicks. The subjects were religious, representing gods, with scenes in the various heavenly abodes or in the different hells. The central figure of each group was about four feet high, and in the background around it were long processions, battles, etc., each figure—and there were hundreds—not over eight or ten inches high. Every detail was most carefully worked out in this large slab of butter, and painted in the florid but painstaking style of lamaist illumination. . . . It takes about three months' labor to finish one of these bas-reliefs, for which the only reward awaiting the makers is the praise of their fellow lamas and a small sum of money given as a prize to the best piece of work. Every year there are new designs and new artists."

[1] "The Border-Land of China," in *The Century Magazine.*

Medallions of clay are given by the Dalai and Tashi Lamas to their worshippers.

There is not much carving done in stone except the six-syllabled sentence, the mystic formula,—

"OM MANI PADME HUM."

This is printed on cotton rags, and flutters from every height; it is rotated in prayer-cylinders; muttered by man, woman, and child, morning, noon, and night; carved on the mountain-side, and on *manis* or prayer-walls; painted on the doors of houses, and engraved on stones. If you ask what it means, no one can tell you, but every one has a most astonishing faith in the efficacy of writing, reading, rotating, and repeating it on every possible occasion and an endless number of times. A literal translation is, *O Jewel in the Lotus! O!* But to

Om Mani Padme Hum.
(Translation; "O jewel in the lotus, O.")
The Lamas' Mystic Sentence Engraved on Stone. On the left is the common form; on the right, the lotus form.

whom the invocation is addressed, and why the mere words should be invested with such extraordinary sanctity and merit-producing power, must remain a mystery. If they think upon the subject at all, probably the Tibetans of to-day consider that they are addressing Avalokita, who is always represented as sitting on a lotus, and his incarnation, the Dalai Lama, whose Tibetan name is Gyal-wa Rin-po-ch'e, "Great Gem of Majesty." The Tashi Lama is also a jewel, his title being Pan-ch'en Rin-po-ch'e, "Great Gem of Learning."

Let us hear Monier Williams: "Whatever be its origin or meaning, no other prayer used by human beings in any quarter of the globe is repeated so often. Every Tibetan believes it to be a panacea for all evil, a compendium of all knowledge, a treasury of all wisdom, a summary of all religion. . . . The real secret of its efficacy lies in the fact that each one of its six syllables has a potent influence on some one of the six gates or 'courses of being';—that is to say, in some one of the six kinds of transmigration through which every living individual has to pass. The oftener, therefore, this mystical formula is repeated, the shorter will be an individual's course through these six forms of existence. It may be he will be able to escape some of the six altogether."

The mysterious words are printed on rolls of

cotton or paper and put into the prayer-cylinders, some of which are great barrels turned by water, wind, or machinery. Others are smaller and placed in rows, like bobbins, with flanges projecting from the spindle below, by which passers-by can give them a turn as they go. They must always be passed to the right, as a mark of respect. One sect of lamas reverses this order, and thus distinguishes itself.

TURNING A PRAYER-DRUM.

"Mani walls" are long, low lines of stone specially erected for the lodgment of slabs with this inscription upon them. It is considered a work of merit to raise such walls. Lamas go about the country chiselling the sentence on rocks or slabs to the order of any man who wants them. They are set up anywhere and in a variety of forms.

In some monasteries there are huge cylinders with a million copies of this mystic prayer revolving inside them. "If," says Mr. Shawe, "you were to introduce steam-power into Tibet to-morrow, probably the first use made of it would be to turn a praying-wheel."

CHAPTER XI

A DEED TO WIN THE EMPIRE

WE are now in a position to appreciate the narrative of Miss Taylor's journey. She trotted into the heart of Tibet, and saw with her own eyes the things we have been describing. She was the first woman traveller to enter the Forbidden Land; and no other European, with one possible, but doubtful, exception, had succeeded in getting so near to Lhasa for more than a generation.

But the real spell of the story lies in the significance of the deed. Miss Taylor's journey changed the whole face of missionary interest in Tibet. It sent a thrill round the world, and is the true beginning of the new and widespread eagerness for the Christian evangelizing of the land. This apparently impregnable Gibraltar of modern missions is now invested on all sides but one, and the siege is being prosecuted with vigor by several societies, working independently of one another, but directed by a common aim and all cheered by the same not distant hope of scaling the impenetrable walls and gaining the confidence of the people.

Let it not be forgotten that the Moravian mission

has been "working and waiting" on the western border for nearly fifty years. Two of the earliest members of that wonderful mission, Mr. and Mrs. Heyde, are still with us and greatly beloved. They ought to be better known for their long and faithful and unostentatious toil. When the day dawns on which the empire of Jesus Christ shall be acknowledged and established in Tibet, they and their colleagues will be honored above all the rest as having laid the foundations and labored the most. Nevertheless, for solitary splendor and sudden quickening power no deed in the whole history will rank higher than this of the lone woman who opened the closed door and deliberately walked through the country, carrying her life in her hands, for Christ's sake and the gospel's.

Miss Taylor started from Tau-chau, on the northern Chinese border. Her plan was to strike through Lhasa and descend to Darjiling. When only within a few days of the holy city, she was stopped, taken prisoner, and forced to retrace her steps. Finally she emerged at Ta-chien-lu, about three hundred miles south of Tau-chau, having chosen a different route from that by which she had come. Altogether, she must have travelled about thirteen hundred miles in the Forbidden Land, and a good piece of this was territory never trodden by white feet before.

It is a pity that exaggerated accounts, due to a want of carefulness on the part of the writers, should have appeared in several religious papers in both England and the United States. One of these, in a glowing passage, hazards the statement: "It has been left for an English young lady to be the first European to enter Tibet proper. This intrepid woman traveller traversed thousands of miles of country where no European foot has ever before trod." Reporters and newspaper correspondents might well claim to be forgiven for blundering on a subject so remote and obscure, but it is different when a book issued under Miss Taylor's own name, and entitled "Pioneering in Tibet," perpetuates this and other misapprehensions. Miss Taylor's achievement is far more impressive when stated simply and in its true proportions.

No European traveller for six and forty years,[1] and no English traveller for over eighty years[2] had come within sight of Lhasa when she took the field. Describe a circle round the city at a radius, say, of one hundred and seventy miles, and you shut them all out. A Russian,[3] in 1885; two Frenchmen,[4] in

[1] Since Huc and Gabet, 1846.

[2] Since Manning, 1811.

[3] Colonel Prejevalsky.

[4] M. Bonvalot and Prince Henry of Orleans, whose narrative is, however, mistrusted to some extent.

1890; an Englishman,[1] in 1891; and an American,[2] in 1892; came approximately near this invisible line, while there is reason to believe that Miss Taylor crossed it and substantially narrowed the cordon. They told her it was three days to Lhasa from the place where they turned her back.[3]

A year after Miss Taylor, two other Frenchmen[4] touched the same point; and, in 1895, an Englishman,[5] with his wife and nephew, reduced the margin to only forty miles. This Englishman, indeed, went to the top of a neighboring hill, and thought to see the city through his glasses, but was doomed to disappointment. Lhasa lies as far off as ever. In 1898 Mr. and Mrs. Rijnhart covered Miss Taylor's track.

Consider another point. Of all these travellers, only two, besides Miss Taylor, undertook the journey alone. Each of the other explorers had a fellow countryman to share with him the risks and toils of the journey. The apparent exceptions were

[1] Captain (now Lieutenant-Colonel) Bower.

[2] Mr. W. W. Rockhill.

[3] We cannot, of course, be certain, on such a datum as this, that Miss Taylor got nearer than the others; the "three days" may mean almost anything according to the speed of travel, but ordinarily it would scarcely stand for a greater distance than one hundred and twenty miles. At any rate, the lady was in the running with the best of them, as they would be delighted to acknowledge.

[4] Messrs. De Rhins and Grenard.

[5] Mr. St. George R. Littledale.

MISS TAYLOR.
Taken at Yatung.

MISS TAYLOR, AS SHE RODE THROUGH TIBET.

OUT FOR A WALK.

Colonel Prejevalsky and Mr. Rockhill. But these were men experienced in Tibetan travel, and provided with adequate material resources for the success of their plan.

It is amusing to contrast Miss Taylor's outfit with that of the rest. Captain Bower was backed by the viceroy of India; he had an officer of the Indian Medical Service assigned him as companion, and was well supplied with servants, animals, and stores.[1] Mr. Knight, who saw him start from Leh, speaks

[1] In his "Diary of a Journey Across Tibet" Captain Bower writes:

"The instruments I decided to take were maximum and minimum thermometers; a three-inch explorer's theodolite, by Cooke; three ordinary thermometers to register low temperatures; hypsometer, by Hicks; with several spare thermometers, bull's-eye lantern, three prismatic compasses, a pocket chronometer, a micrometer, several pocket compasses, and three aneroids. These, with sheets of drying-paper between wire frames, and arsenical soap, to hold botanical and for natural history specimens respectively, made up the scientific equipment of the expedition.

"As regards medicines we took an 'Army Railway Medical Companion,' to which were added a few medicines for diseases of the eye, vaseline, and iodoform; vaseline is an absolute essential, as on the plateaux of Central Asia, owing to the high winds and extreme dryness, the skin of the hands and face gets terribly chapped, while mixed with iodoform it makes an absolutely perfect dressing for horses' sore backs. I would advise future travellers in those regions to take some paregoric as well, as colds and coughs have to be guarded against.

"For clothing we equipped ourselves in thick putto, a sort of native woollen cloth made in Kashmir, with warm woollen underclothing, and sheepskin robes. Our boots were the ordinary infantry ammunition pattern made a good deal too large, so as to be able to wear several pairs of thick woollen socks; the latter were

of the "princely equipage of Bower." I do not know what Prejevalsky considered necessary for his

all made of double thickness at the toes and heels. A dozen chamois-leather skins for patching clothes were also taken.

"For bedding we had felts, lambskin rugs, and blankets; blankets alone are of little use against great cold, and no amount of woollen clothes will keep out the wind on the Chang (Central Tibetan plateau); so skins must be taken.

"Our battery consisted of two double-barrelled five hundred express rifles, one twelve-bore shotgun, two cavalry regulation carbines, and three revolvers. We had about three hundred rounds for the express rifles, two hundred for the shotgun, mostly No. 6; two hundred for the carbines, and one or two packets of revolver ammunition.

"Dr. Thorold and myself rode on troopers' saddles. These have great advantage over ordinary hunting-saddles; in the first place, a carbine can be carried in the bucket, and so is always handy for defence. The chances are that it may never be required for that purpose; but, if it is required, it is required very badly, and if carried anywhere else is almost certain not to be handy at the right moment. Besides, when riding along, should a chance of shooting an antelope occur, as continually happens at the most unexpected moments, one has it handy. Moreover, a trooper's saddle will easily carry a great-coat, lunch, field-glasses, etc.

"It is absolutely necessary to have some literature on these sorts of expeditions, as the mind yearns for food. Books being heavy and transport limited, nothing that will not bear rereading should be taken. Our library consisted of Shakespeare, Napier's 'Peninsular War,' and Carlyle's 'Sartor Resartus.' Books, instruments, and clothes were all stowed in Kashmir-made leather-bound yakdans, two of which formed General Kinloch's pattern bed, and were long enough to hold gun-barrels. Our tents consisted of a sepoy's pal (a tent with the roof sloping down to the ground, and no side walls), ten feet long and six feet high; one slightly longer for the caravan-drivers; the inside of an eighty pound Kabul tent; and a tente d'abri to serve as kitchen; all were of cotton, and except the last they were lined with putto; but I am inclined to think that an extra cotton lining would be a more effectual protection against the wind."

swoop on the Lhasa district, but Mr. Rockhill says that his equipment on a former expedition in eastern Tibet comprised fourteen Cossacks and sixty-five camels. The Littledales were quite an armed caravan. "My scheme was," says Mr. Littledale, "to strain every nerve to reach Tibet, and, if possible, Lhasa, with plenty of food and animals to carry it. Most of the other expeditions had failed owing to their arriving in a more or less destitute condition; and then, of course, the Tibetans could dictate their own terms. We also relied upon bribery, and went well prepared with the sinews of war for wholesale corruption."[1]

What with sepoys, express rifles, and "lightning repeaters," they were able to play a good game of bluff before giving in; but all the same they had to give in. Even the Rijnharts took with them two years' provisions.

Miss Taylor started with ten horses, two tents, and food for two months, principally tsamba or barley-flour. She had a camp-bed and a box with "presents for chiefs." A few ounces of silver and some Chinese cotton cloth constituted her slender exchequer. She also took a few English clothes to be worn on arrival in India. Her kit for the table consisted of two tin basins, a wooden bowl or two, and a copper pan, together with knife, fork, and

[1] *The Geographical Journal*, May, 1896.

spoon. All these goods fell into the hands of chuk-pa (brigands), and for the most part she had to do without them. Amongst the stolen things which were never recovered was a parcel of Tibetan Gospels. Who can tell into what nooks and corners of the land these have been carried since? Her library consisted of four books, kept in the folds of her sheepskin gown: 1. "Daily Light" (Morning Hour). 2. The New Testament and Psalms. 3. An English hymn-book. 4. A notebook for the diary.

For twenty nights she slept in the open air. A cave would have been a luxury. For months she could not change her clothes. Of the three Chinamen who accompanied her, one turned back, another died on the road, and the third tried to take her life. A Tibetan youth, Pontso, followed her through it all to the end.

If the achievement was unique, so, too, was the motive. Miss Taylor aimed at opening a way for the gospel; her simple notion was to march through the closed land and claim it for God. It would be difficult, of course; that she understood, but she refused to believe that the difficulties were insuperable. She argued that we have received no orders from the Lord which are impossible to be carried out. He has bidden us go into all the world and preach the gospel to every creature.

There is something whimsical in the thought of this weak woman leading in her tiny expedition accomplish so great an object. But who can withhold admiration for the calm courage and unquestioning faith that could thus press forward, keeping its secret in its bosom, and absolutely sure of final success? With a confidence which has since been vindicated she told herself that she was doing a great work for the Christianizing of Tibet. And the consciousness that God had sent her to do it is the key to that buoyancy of spirit which lightens all the story and never shines more brightly than when she is face to face with death.

"I am God's little woman, and he will take care of me," she writes. On another occasion: "All must be well with the ambassadors of the Lord. I am his charge."

Finding the Yellow River too swollen to be crossed, she sits down quietly to wait till the water subsides. There is no chafing, no trace of impatience or doubt. What she whispers to herself is very different, and shows a rare serenity:—"The Lord can do this for me. My eyes are unto Him who made a passage in the Red Sea for the children of Israel."

When one of the Chinamen, Leucotze, a man of great strength, succumbed to the cold, she buried him with the words, "The Master has called to account the strong, and left the weak to go on and claim Tibet in his name."

"God will take care of us," she is constantly saying, till it is almost like the refrain of some sweet song stilling the heart. And every little beam of brightness, every easing of the circumstances, rough and cheerless though they were at the best, calls for faithful and loving recognition. "The Lord does indeed take care of us," she writes; and you feel that this is not cant; it is childlike confidence, and the consciousness of "very present help," which calms and cheers the mind.

As they neared Lhasa, and the supreme crisis drew near, the two Tibetans—all that was left to her of escort and protection—grew more and more afraid. "The hardest thing I have to bear," she said, "is their fears." On in front, waiting to waylay them, was the Chinese guide. They were shelterless and hard pressed in the heart of a hostile land. All around were foes. Within were the gravest misgivings. But the lonely traveller looked up through the gloom to God, and pillowed her head on words which have voiced the faith of thousands of Christian hearts:—

> "All my trust on thee is stayed,
> All my help from thee I bring;
> Cover my defenceless head
> With the shadow of thy wing."

It is one thing to sing these words in the company of the redeemed and in the loving shelter of the home or the church; but to trace them under the Tibetan sky, with darkness around, and death creeping near in the darkness, is quite another. It is courage of the highest kind that could so support a feeble woman, and enable her, not only to master her own fears, but to inspire those greater weaklings, the two men, her servants, with sufficient spirit to proceed.

If you imagine, because of these extracts, that Miss Taylor's narrative is a record of religious emotion, or a diary of devout sentiments, you do not know anything about it.

"Quite safe here with Jesus," she writes; and I confess the phrase makes me wince, but the face above the pencil is rosy and roguish, and the picture is that of a busy little gypsy boiling her obstinate Christmas pudding under the lee of the hill. In truth, she is genuinely human all the way through. There is no mistaking a certain high relish for the life. She enjoys riding and roughing it on her romantic journey. There is a humorous side to the venture, which she is quick to see, and she laughs over it merrily as she jogs along.

Moreover, all the resources of her woman's wit are called into play. Whether it be foiling the feints of her faithless guide or checking the moves of the Nag-chu-ka chief, she searches with a keen feminine eye the delinquencies of unregenerate man. She has her own little wiles, too, which seldom fail to succeed. When challenged and opposed, her will, within certain limits, was inflexible, it was almost defiant. Do they think to tame her or crush her spirit? She will show them they are greatly mistaken. She will make no answer to an impudent magistrate till he has changed his tone, and she utterly refuses to dismount and bow down when they pass the great lamaseries on the road. All the same, this indomitable temper is most naturally blended with a blind abandonment of herself and her fate to the guidance of specious pretenders. Quite naturally, too, when their rascality is discovered, and the villains whimper a little, she is ready to restore them to favor if they promise to be good.

The subordinate characters in this artless narrative are alive and entertaining. There is Noga, the Chinese guide, greedy of gain, yet more and more disliking his task, and dreading the inevitable consequence of taking a foreigner into Tibet. He dissembled from the beginning, but that is the Chinaman's way. It is difficult to decide whether he ever really meant to fulfil his contract and lead the stranger to Lhasa. At an early stage he developed active opposition, and after that did his best to thwart the plan. Finally, he turned traitor, and caused the traveller's arrest.

Then comes Pontso, the Tibetan page, still more fearful, as he had need to be, but faithful, and perhaps a little pampered. The key to the course of events is the play of jealous passion between these two. Pontso was an old servant; he had accompanied Miss Taylor by sea from India, and thence through China into Tibet; and it was natural that he should be more trusted than the other. He was also a professing Christian.

But Noga was incomparably the abler and more powerful, and it was probably mistaken policy to slight him. He appears to have specially resented being called a "servant," and there were frequent disputes as to the nature of the agreement by which he was bound. It is charitable to suppose that there may have been on his part, at least, some misunderstanding of the terms.

Noga, leading the way, and Pontso, riding beside his mistress, were followed by a third man whose duty lay with the pack-horses lingering in the rear. None of these animals survived the march, and Leucotze himself yielded up his life. He was thought to be lazy, and was certainly absent-minded, as when he carefully led a dog's rope over the river without the dog! but his last breath was a cry to Allah, and his last resting-place a wet grave in the snow-sodden soil.

Penting took his place, an escort and drover engaged on the road, Penting the good-hearted, the tearful, aware of his peril in such company, and specially apprehensive of retribution to be visited by the authorities upon his wife and children, but acting his part faithfully to the end. As defender of his mistress's life he was without reproach; as defrauding her of goods and chattels he was without a rival.

Miss Taylor was twice under fire. The first time she came upon the chuk-pa unawares. They were off their horses, squatting on the ground, and quietly drinking tea. It took them some time to light up their tinder and mount their horses, and then the surprise—or was it the tea?—made their matchlocks wabble; for, though they blazed away with a will, little damage was done. But it was rather a frightening experience. The second time, a force of two hundred bandits surrounded our feeble party in what was almost a *cul de sac*, and the whistling bullets spattered the stones with blood. They were travelling with a company of Mongols and laden yaks. The beasts stampeded; several of them were shot, and with them fell two men, face downwards, whose muffled bodies were left lying still and cold for the oncoming night to cover and the pitiless rain to pelt.

The story reaches its climax at the trial scene three days from Lhasa. For fifteen days after her arrest Miss Taylor stood at bay, fighting for her life and the lives of the two Tibetans. There were several preliminary hearings by inferior chiefs, and finally the biggest man of all travelled from Nag-chu-ka to try the case.

A great tent was put up, a white tent with a device in blue sewn across the front. The inside was draped with curtains. At one end sat the chiefs on high cushions, cross-legged. The higher the chief, the higher the cushion. A tea-table stood in front of each, with a china cup for tea. Close by was a brazier of lurid coals. A servant kept replenishing the teacups from a kettle on the fire. It all looked very homely and reassuring. But the prisoners knew better. They knew that their fate hung on the judgment of those tea-drinking chiefs. The back of the tent was crowded with soldiers and servants.

In the centre sat the woman on whose account all this fuss was being made,—a foreigner, and therefore guilty of criminal trespass; a prisoner, unarmed, and absolutely without provisions. It is impossible not to admire the unflinching courage and resourcefulness of her tactics in the presence of so many curious and unfriendly eyes. She turned the tables on her informer, and actually succeeded in wresting from him her stolen property, so skilfully did she conduct her defence. And, although she failed to get permission to go to Lhasa, or to pass by it to Darjiling, she wrung from the chiefs, as compensation for this refusal, a tent, horses, and provisions sufficient for the return to China.

Then she toiled back, more dead than alive, and after many and new adventures arrived at Ta-chien-lu on the thirteenth of April, 1893, having spent the worst months of the year in the interior of Tibet.

When the news reached England, and still more when the traveller herself appeared, and began to tell her tale, intense interest was aroused in this last unoccupied stronghold of the heathen world. Meetings were held among the churches, and much prayer began to be made. Within a very short time a band of men "whose hearts the Lord had touched" placed themselves under her leadership to live and die for Tibet. Thus was formed the "Tibetan Pioneer Mission," which sailed for India immediately, hoping to enter the land through the Sikkim gates.

The choice of a name was unfortunate, because amongst those unacquainted with the facts it lent

THE "TIBETAN PIONEER MISSION."
Taken at Darjiling in 1894

color to the erroneous supposition that now for the first time was work going to be done for Tibet. The real "pioneers" here, as in so many other hard and sterile fields, were the noble Moravians, who had already been toiling for thirty-seven years on the Tibetan border, and purely for Tibetans, when Miss Taylor made her eventful journey. They had translated the Scriptures, and prepared many books in the language of the people, those very Gospels which Miss Taylor carried into the interior being the fruit of their work.[1] The name was probably intended rather to describe the character of the mission than its chronological position. It was hoped that its members would soon find access to the country and move about freely within it as pioneers, preparing the way for more regular and established work.

But a different result ensued. Of those who reached India, all but one, after a few months' trial, seceded from their leader. It was unhappy, but it was inevitable. There were incompatible elements in their mutual relations which ought to have been foreseen and more wisely adjusted. Some regrettable circumstances notwithstanding, it would be very unjust, I think, to blame them

[1] No account is here taken of the Roman Catholic missions on the Chinese border, which have existed for centuries and from which many friars have entered and passed through the land.

for the act of withdrawal. Separation was best in every way. It was doubtless a deep disappointment to all concerned, and not least to Miss Taylor, when the mission dissolved; but God has given her a better thing than the thing she wanted to have. He has scattered the band that he might use it in a wider sphere and fit it for better work.

Two of the original members are dead. Two more[1] are happily at work with the Scotch mission at Kalimpong. They have a splendid field. Kalimpong is the main base of Tibetan trade with Bengal, and hundreds of Tibetans camp there in the cold season every year. The rest of the members, with perhaps one exception, are all in China[2] and all working for Tibet, engaged in developing an active and far-reaching evangelistic campaign along the whole of its eastern border, under the experienced leadership of Mr. Cecil Polhill Turner.

Thus the skirmishing force that would have been choked and helpless, cooped up in the gorge at Yatung, has wheeled off south and east, and is touching the country at a dozen points with immensely greater promise of effective attack.

Yet it cannot be forgotten that the impulse which

[1] Mr. and Mrs. Evan Mackenzie.

[2] Or were when this page was written. Since then the troublous state of the country has disorganized their plans and driven them for a time from the field.

created that mobile and gallant little army was the impulse given by the Spirit of God under the simple recital of Miss Taylor's story, the story of her wonderful journey into the heart of Tibet. Nor is this all. It was that journey which fired the imagination of the Rijnharts, and led them, five years later, to make the same attempt; and their story, with its tragic mystery and speechless pain, has been a new and most powerful appeal to the sympathies and intercession of the Christian world.

CHAPTER XII

FIRST CONTACT WITH THE TIBETANS

MISS TAYLOR was born at Egremont, Cheshire, on the seventeenth of October, 1855. She was therefore just thirty-six when she made her famous journey.

Her father, Mr. John Taylor, is said to have spent the greater part of a long life wandering about the world. She herself was early bitten with the same love of travel, and has had a remarkable career.

As a child she was one of those weaklings "not expected to live" who have afterwards exhibited robust vigor and endured hardships which would put a strain on nerves of steel. It is amusing to read of "valvular disease of the heart," chronic bronchitis, and general hopelessness of health, as descriptive of the constitution of the only woman traveller who has ventured alone into Tibet.

She struggled through her teens with difficulty and but little schooling—who could discipline so delicate a child? and, being largely left to her own devices, discovered a wilfulness that was happily softened and sanctified by early consecration to

God. At the close of a quiet service one Sunday evening, in the quaint little town of Kingston on Thames, the girl of thirteen knelt down and yielded herself to the Lord Jesus Christ. "He died for *me*"—that was the thought that thrilled her soul and swept away past offences. Then came its complement of perfect comfort, "He *lives* for me—Jesus, my Saviour, my constant and closest Friend"—and that thought has been with her, sweet as ointment poured forth, through all the after years.

But there was a conflict waiting for the young disciple, and a cross for her to carry, amongst her own people and in her father's house. She was the eldest but one of ten children, and had a liberal allowance of money to spend as she pleased. The step she had taken was misunderstood, and it led to decisions in detail which were much resented. She acted, as she believed, in obedience to the heavenly vision, but her conduct appeared as mere obstinate clinging to a course which the rest of the family disapproved. She refused to ride out on Sundays, came to dislike the theatre, and ceased to dance.

At various places in England and on the Continent she attended school, or took lessons in painting, for short periods during the intervals of better health. The call to be a missionary came at Clarence House,

Richmond, as she listened to an address on Africa and the work of Dr. Moffat, given by his son. The appeal made was for *men;* and the schoolgirl, "for the only time in my life," as she naïvely tells us, regretted the disabilities of sex.

Twelve years passed before the dream which then began to haunt her thoughts was fulfilled. In the mean time, she did what she could, visiting the sick in Brighton, and afterwards taking a London district. Her ideal seems to have been a gentle, self-sacrificing lady who afterwards became the wife of Dr. Barnardo, and whose fellowship and sympathy was her greatest encouragement.

At twenty-eight the crisis came. Father and daughter had a frank but sorrowful talk. The old battle was fought over again. He required her to renounce Christian work, and she on her part as steadily refused. Finally, he gave an ironical consent to her missionary plans, of which she availed herself immediately by entering one of the London hospitals for an elementary medical course. But the consent was immediately withdrawn, and there was soon an open rupture at home. Allowances ceased. She sold her jewels, and with the proceeds paid her way at the hospital, while supporting herself in cheap lodgings, till a reconciliation took place. Happily that was soon effected, for Mrs. Taylor had spent a winter in Sicily, and the comforts of Christ had come to her in a little Italian chapel within sound of the sea. Thereafter there were two that perfectly understood each other, mother and child, and the family life was changed.

In the month of October, 1884, Miss Taylor sailed for China, under direction of the China Inland Mission. Her father so far countenanced the plan as to provide her with an ample outfit; and, believing she would soon tire of missionary work, he gave her letters of authorization to the great steamship companies at Shanghai, as a means of covering her retreat. But he also stopped her allowance, not considering it seemly to sanction refractory ways.

Miss Taylor spent three years in China; first at Chin-kiang, in the estuary of the Yang-tse-Kiang; then at Gan-king, in the province of Gan-Hwuy; and, finally, far away north of the Koko-Nor, between the great wall and the Tibetan border, at Liang-Chau, the capital of Kan-su. Here she did medical work of a homely kind among the Chinese officials, and began to think longingly of Tibet.

From a child that mysterious land had exercised a strange fascination over her mind. And now she was very near it, within sight of its snowy crests, within touch of its people as they crossed the border for purposes of trade. She determined to use the opportunity, and attend the great Tibetan fair which is held near Si-ning, at the famous Kumbum Monastery to which reference has already been made.[1]

Lieutenant-Colonel Bower says, "Mr. Rockhill probably knows more about Tibet than any other living man." Mr. Rockhill first saw Kumbum in February, 1889. But Miss Taylor was before him. She was there in July, 1887. I have at my elbow, as I write, the handful of crumpled wax-sheets on which she traced the story of her visit, illustrated by quaint marginal sketches, amongst which "a Tibetan man," "a Tibetan woman," and "a lama" figure very prominently. It is interesting as recording her first impressions of that sturdy but enslaved race for which she was afterwards to dare so much.

VISIT TO A TIBETAN FAIR HELD IN TA'RI'SI[2]

KUMBUM MONASTERY, JULY, 1887.

"Ta'ri'si, one of the large lamaseries of Tibet, is fifty li from Si-ning and adjoins the Chinese town Lusar. It contains between two and three thousand lamas. It is the birthplace of Tson K'apa, who in the fifteenth century reformed and established the worship of Buddha in Tibet, in its present form.

[1] For an able description of this monastery see "The Border-Land of China," by Mr. W. W. Rockhill, *The Century Magazine*, Vol. XLI., 33.

[2] Miss Taylor's Ta'ri'si (Ta'-erh-ssu, the great tabernacle) is the Mongolian name for the Kumbum Monastery.

It is also the residence of the living representative of Buddha. When one representative dies, the lamas go on a pilgrimage until they find a baby boy born at the same time. They bring the baby to the lamasery, and show him the possessions of the late Buddha. If he smiles, it shows that he recognizes the things, and is therefore the living embodiment; but, if not, they have to continue the search until they find the right one.

"Ta'ri'si was destroyed and sacked during the Mohammedan rebellion in 1867, before which time it contained four thousand lamas, and was much more imposing. The chief temple was then roofed with gold plates, whereas the roof is now gilt brass.

"The temples, which are numerous, are solid-looking buildings. They are lofty, and have a row of windows near the top. They are probably built after an Indian order of architecture, as they have no resemblance to the Chinese. The houses of the lamas are like the Chinese, with the one exception that they are scrupulously clean, whereas the Chinese are dreadfully dirty. The rooms are built round a courtyard; they have trellis-work windows with thin paper pasted over them. The rooms have brick beds with wooden planks laid across the top, which lift up, and a fire of dried cow-dung is let inside to heat the bed.

"The lamas live, or are supposed to live, a life of

celibacy. The eldest son of every Tibetan family is set apart for the priesthood. They are evidently sent to the lamasery about the age of ten, and there they are taught to read, but all seem to spend some of their time at home. They, like their seniors, have their heads shaved, and wear a full skirt of red cotton or woollen cloth, and a sleeveless body, open in front, with a stand-up collar; the body falls over the skirt and is gathered in at the waist by a girdle; over all they throw a scarf about a yard and a half broad and four yards long, most gracefully draping the shoulders and concealing the hands and arms. Their boots are high, and made of red cloth like the rest of the dress.

"The lamas are governed by four kalon or secular rulers, who reside at the different lamaseries. I twice saw the one who lives in Ta'ri'si; he looks between fifty and sixty, and is evidently accustomed to being obeyed. The first time he was inspecting the embankment round the lamasery, which the lamas were mending; and the next time he was walking through the fair with two lamas walking before him and clearing the way with two whips with long leather lashes. He was dressed only a little better than the others. The lamas are not at all intellectual-looking; they go about telling their beads, with a little dog.

"The Tibetans are a muscular, well-built race;

they have small eyes, high cheek-bones, prominent noses, and large mouths. The men have their heads and faces clean-shaved as a rule. They wear a garment of coarse woollen serge, or sheepskin (with the wool inside), down to the knees, and tied round the waist with a girdle. When in the saddle they take their arms out of the sleeves, and let the garment hang over the girdle. They wear cotton trousers and high leather Wellington boots; their cap has a sheepskin border and a red and blue cotton centre; it fits tightly to the head. They have a sword hanging at their side, and also a knife, which they use for eating their food; and when travelling they carry a rough sort of gun.[1]

"The women are shorter than the men and broadset. They wear only one garment, a dress of dark-blue serge bordered with red; it has a large turn-back sheepskin collar. There are no fastenings to the dress, but it folds over in front, and is kept on by a girdle. When working, they take the right arm out of the sleeve, exposing the breast. Their gala dress is a large,

WOMAN IN GALA DRESS

WOMAN IN USUAL DRESS

[1] The Tibetan gun is a matchlock with a long pair of prongs hinged to the barrel, on which they rest the weapon to keep it steady and aid them in shooting straight.

elaborate, stiff sort of sacking; it is embroidered with colored silks, and in the centre are three embossed silver ornaments about two inches in diameter, and round the edges opaque pieces of shells (oyster-shells, I should think), and beads of carnelian. Their wrists are covered with strings of stone, coral, and glass beads. They wear silver and gold earrings. One I noticed was a silver ring with red coral stones, and a string of coral beads attached from one earring to the other. On state occasions the women wear boots like the men, but generally go barefoot. They do their hair up into a number of little plaits,—one woman had sixty-four—and these are caught at the bottom in a piece of cloth folded like a bag, and sewn across the top. Some have one large plait of twenty in the centre, and small ones on each side. They wear the same sort of hats as the men.

"The fair is held on the hill between Lusar and Ta'ri'si. There were two streets of stalls kept by Chinamen. Some were drapers who sold foreign and Chinese stuffs and ribbons, and Chinese satin caps, like those of the men, only a little more fanciful, which the Tibetan women bought and wore. Haberdashers were there with cottons, needles, buttons, looking-glasses, combs, beads, and all kinds of ornaments for the women's sashes, as well as embroidery, silk, and cottons. Braziers had their saucepans, lamps, and the different brass articles used in worship. Ironmongers had iron saucepans, knives, nails, and the point for the wooden ploughs. There were stalls of incense, done up in packets. Most popular of all, perhaps, were the tents in which food both cooked and uncooked was sold, as well as Chinese spirit. The Tibetans indulged themselves greedily. In the evenings they had drinking-bouts, in which the women joined; they sat in a ring on the hill and sang songs. Drinking is one of the evil habits the civilized Chinese have taught the Tibetans. On the hillside wooden buckets, tubs, and churns were offered for sale. The Tibetans were selling coarse woollen stuff made by themselves, and little wooden basins they use to eat out of; also wool and large numbers of sheep, horses, and other cattle. I found that a bullock for field work cost about a pound, English money, but for food from five to ten shillings. A sheep fetched one shilling or less, a horse about a pound; but one could be got for ten shillings. Wool was worth five shillings a hundredweight. These are the prices if one buys directly from the Tibetans.

"The Tibetans were encamped on the hills, with their cattle round them, and the wool in stacks in the centre. I visited many of the encampments; some were quite a distance from the fair. The tents are mostly white and like those we are accustomed to see in England. They have no furniture in them, the Tibetans sleeping on bundles of wool or on the ground. The cooking-utensils consist of a large copper saucepan, a wooden ladle, and a pair of bellows, made of sheepskin, with a long iron pipe, which they keep blowing all the time the pan is on the fire. The fuel is brushwood.

"Their food is peculiar and coarse; they boil a little brick tea in plenty of water; then add butter, ladling the broth into basins and working in barley-meal until it is a stiff paste, when they eat it with their fingers. Sometimes they make a sort of soup with meal and pieces of raw mutton, which when barely warmed through are taken out and eaten. A knife is used when the meat will not come away from the bones. A dear old Tibetan man, from whom I bought two wooden bowls for threepence, showed me his stock of provisions; they were done up in leather bags. He had barley-meal, dried peas, a sort of biscuit in small pieces, made of flour and water, a skin with some very rancid butter in it, and a little brick tea.

"Tibet, by what I hear, is practically a grazing country, but many of the Tibetans have settled in farms on the Chinese border. These put on Chinese dress and speak Chinese, as they say they can thus make better bargains. The cattle and camels that had come to the fair with wool from Tibet took back leather sacks full of flour or barley-meal. The hills and country round Ta'ri'si are beautifully green, as it often rains; but vegetation is backward on account of the cold. Any one who could live on mutton, milk, and butter would fare well in Tibet. Vegetables are scarce, and fruit still more so. Mutton was a little over, and beef a little less than, a penny a pound. Fowls were threepence each, eggs fourteen a penny, and six little loaves of bread, each as large as an English halfpenny roll, cost a penny; milk was three farthings a quart. House-rent is not dear, for a Mohammedan who is friendly with the Tibetans told me that he could get me a small house in a Tibetan village for tenpence a month. Up to about two days' journey from Ta'ri'si the Tibetans have houses built like the Chinese, but beyond that they live in mud huts without windows and with only a curtain for the door. They are well protected by large, fierce dogs, fed on sheep's blood.

"A Mohammedan, with whose family I was soon on good terms, told me a little about the Tibetans. His father and grandfather are cattle-dealers. They go into Tibet to buy cattle, and stay some days at the different places. A few Tibetans were paying a return visit at their house. There was an unmarried girl of twenty, also her father and grandfather and two other men; they all slept together in one little room.[1] The old man would not let his granddaughter eat some Chinese cakes I gave her, saying to me in Chinese, "You cannot speak our words, so she must not eat your cakes." She could not speak Chinese.

"A Tibetan girl does not marry unless she likes. One woman has often three or four husbands. The men seem fond of their wives, taking their hands and making them walk in front. They laugh and talk together—so different from the Chinese. The women are afraid of strangers. They would often run away when I approached, and one man nearly struck me when I offered a text-card to his little wife. They thought at first that I was a man, because my ears are not pierced. But I soon made friends, and then they would invite me to sit in the midst of them on the hillside. Some came to see me in the inn.

"My room was one of a row of little pigeon-boxes built on the roof, which is slanted. It had no furniture in it but a brick bed, my rights to which were disputed by its small inhabitants. We made a fire of brushwood on the roof, as we had to do our own cooking. The inn was very dirty.

"The Chinese call the Tibetans wild people, and in the evenings, when I visited the encampments, my servant was afraid they would kill me; but

[1] This is the rule in Tibet.

they let me sit amongst them while they cooked and ate their food, and then received the text-cards. I longed to be able to speak to them, but I managed to pick up only a few Tibetan words.

"The Tibetans are a religious people. The men and women all wear a casket round the neck next the skin. It is made of brass, and has an idol inside. I was shocked to see men and women near Ta'ri'si, prostrating themselves the whole length of the road. They fold their hands together, and place them before the forehead and before the breast, then fall flat on the ground, touching the earth with their foreheads, and, stretching their hands beyond the head, make a mark on the ground. After this they get up, and put their feet on the mark, and again prostrate themselves, until they have done the whole round of the lamasery boundary. The women devotees went barefoot, and their faces and dress were all begrimed with dirt. They were repeating prayers the whole time. Poor things, they know no better; no one has ever told them of Jesus. There are little temples in the different corners of the road. Some of these are decorated with paintings of goddesses in white, red, yellow, and black. Some have a group of gods surrounding a prayer-wheel, which all the pilgrims set in motion as they pass. Some walk round the temple two or three times, giving the wheel a turn each time.

"I visited one of the largest temples in Ta'ri'si. Some Tibetan women, having paid me a visit in the inn and tasted my tea and cakes,[1] invited me in return to go with them and see the temple. We first passed through a courtyard on the sides of which were pictures of gods. The temple had two black doors garnished with painted skulls.[2] Inside it was hung with banners and tiger-skins. The effect was very sombre. Facing the door stood a table, on which were lighted butter lamps and round brass basins full of clear cold water. Behind it was a curtain; on one side there was a stuffed tiger in a springing position and a small black bear; on the other side were another tiger and a sort of black goat or deer, with butter lamps. In front were plaster figures of demons. One was represented as surrounded by flames of fire, and there were painted skeletons in white on the walls. The people bowed down before the images, but behind the door were some lamas drinking tea and enjoying themselves.

[1] Miss Taylor is a skilful cook. The members of her family used to tell her teasingly it was her *one* talent.

[2] Mr. Rockhill, speaking of the "Treasure House," says, "On the panels of the gates were painted human skins, the hands, feet, and head hanging to them and all reeking with blood—these to frighten all evil-doers, most likely, and make their flesh creep at the very thought of what might befall them if they tried to rob the place." —"Border-Land of China," p. 254.

They say there is a famous teapot in the temple as big as a small room, which they use at festivals. I did not see it.

"I went on to a smaller temple in which were gilt or brass images of Buddha. A lama was sitting beside them and attending to the butter lamps. The visitors here put cash on the table in front of the idols. There was to have been a lama dance (masquerade) on the fifth day of the fair, but it did not take place.

"On the sixth day there was a procession. As we were passing by the skulls on the floor, a woman asked me to look at the arm of her little child. It had been scalded the previous evening, and was one mass of blisters. They had partially covered it with fresh cow-dung. At my request they got some linseed oil and flour, which were easily procurable, and I dressed the arm. The mother was very grateful, and I think I got a little nearer the hearts of the Tibetans and lamas who were looking on.

"We then hurried on and reached the entrance of Ta'ri'si just as the procession was leaving the lamasery. First came some plain lamas, then two others blowing horns about six feet long. I think the horns were made of copper. They gave forth a deep, rich sound. Then a number of lamas carrying banners. The cloth was draped round a small circle at the top of the pole. Six were white with a black stripe, which gave the appearance of a cross. The lamas had large yellow helmets on their heads, made of wool cut like velvet, with a thick fringe standing up at the top. They looked very imposing. After them came the Buddha. He had a gold mitre on his head, and a long cloak of gold cloth. When the crowd pressed round, a lama sprang forward and drove them back with a whip. I saw a girl and a boy, who were hurt, crying bitterly."

Here the narrative breaks off, some of the sheets being missing; but the portion preserved is characteristic. There is the same cheerful spirit that sustained her during the long journey five years later; the same pair of wide-awake eyes, not without a twinkle in them; the same warmly sympathetic heart, and a manner full of engaging frankness, which brought her easily and quickly into friendly relations with all sorts of people.

The year after her visit to Kumbum Miss Taylor was forced down country by illness. On the way, she was wrecked in the rapids of the Han. The boatmen had been drinking over night, and the boat was smashed against the rocks, and sunk. But at last she reached the coast.

Her father was travelling in Australia, and she

joined him to recruit her health. From Australia they came to England, taking Darjiling on the way. This established the cure, and she was soon again in India with the object of reaching the Tibetans from the Indian side. At Ghûm, near Darjiling, she lived for five months in a native hut, and in March, 1890, moved over the border to the Sachen valley in Sikkim.

But her presence was obnoxious to the authorities, and she was ordered to leave the valley. The captain of the guard of the Dong-kya Pass came over from the Chinese fort at Khamba-jong to settle what should be done. Finally she was moved to Tumlong, and given a room in the monastery there. But the people had been told not to sell her any food, and she found it difficult to live. On one occasion she followed a caravan over the stony roads, and eased her hunger a little by picking up the grains of parched corn which dribbled through a small hole in one of the packs carried by a mule.

It was while at this monastery that she first saw Pontso. He was a Lhasa youth, about nineteen years of age, who had run away from his master in Tibet. He came to her for treatment, with some disease of the foot, and afterwards became her servant, following her faithfully through all her travels in Tibet.

Miss Taylor's sojourn in Sikkim did her one

great service. It enabled her to speak Tibetan as it is spoken at Lhasa. But there was no opening into the lamas' land.

One evening, in March, 1891, she was writing her letters when suddenly a voice seemed to say to her, "Go to China." It was remarkable, too, that on that very evening a postal notice reached her, indicating the dates for the sailing of the Chinese mail from Calcutta. She started immediately, went down to Calcutta, and took ship for China. But she feared she would have to wait a long time at the coast, that it would be too late in the year to pass through the rapids and travel to the Tibetan border. Pontso was with her. The missionaries at Shanghai advised her to take him no further, as he was sure to be beheaded. They started up country, and were carried over the rapids, by a swelling of the waters, with a sudden rush.[1] The next party was delayed three months in getting through. At Chin-shan Pontso got very ill, and his funeral was arranged for. But he recovered. The two went on to open the city of Tau-chau, and within a fortnight secured a house. They were there a year, and then they tramped through Tibet!

[1] It is not to be too hastily assumed from this and similar occurrences that Providence favors only the good. God "sendeth rain on the just and on the unjust." Even in this instance there were two boats that were rushed through; one was Miss Taylor's, but the other had a cargo of spirits.

CHAPTER XIII

TRANSCRIBING THE DIARY

WHEN I visited Yatung in July, 1899, I had not the remotest intention of editing Miss Taylor's diary. I was not even aware of its existence. The meagre summary of her adventures published in that disappointing booklet, "Pioneering in Tibet," contained no suggestion of fuller sources from which a more adequate account might some day be written.

I was accompanied by Mr. A. Stafford Crawley, then private secretary to Bishop Welldon, and for both of us it was just a holiday jaunt and nothing more. This is not the place in which to recount our adventures, but the opportunity may perhaps present itself on a later occasion. In spite of depressing weather, the worst swelter and scour of the rains, we enjoyed the trip, and especially the glimpse it gave us of the Tibetan question on Tibetan ground.

It was a new, not to say an exhilarating, sensation to find ourselves one morning roaming about in the Forbidden Land, and being scowled back with the usual cutthroat gestures.

Then there were Miss Taylor and her story, and her "shop," and all the problems that arise out of these, full of intensest interest. We found her a strange complexity of daring, devotion, and diplomacy. I do not wonder that the government regarded her as a thorn in its side. We listened for hours as she chatted over the teacups in her little box of a room, slowly taking in the perspective of the story with all the advantage of a natural background and local color. This much was clear, that she had consecrated her life without stint to the service of Jesus Christ, on behalf of Tibet, and had succeeded in bringing the claims of that hard field very closely home to the Christian heart.

Nothing was so important, from this point of view, as the wonderful journey which she undertook and accomplished in 1892-93. Was there no better record of it than that which had already appeared? Had no journal been kept? Had she made no notes as she went along? These questions I sought an opportunity of asking, and for answer Miss Taylor opened a drawer and took out a black notebook with faded red edges, much besmeared and soiled with dirt and wet.

"This," she said, "is my diary. I carried it in my dress all the way to Nag-chu-ka and back, and wrote in it every day. But the writing is so illegible that I doubt if anybody could read it. I have the greatest difficulty in reading it myself. There are parts which I cannot make out at all."

I handled the book gently, and not without a feeling of reverence as I thought of the brave woman who amidst all her hardships had committed her way unto the Lord and her heart's secrets of faith and fear to these unresponsive pages. I did not attempt to read what was written. Delicacy forbade that a stranger should pry into that private record. I gave the book back, and the next day we left Yatung.

In the course of subsequent correspondence, when the idea of a missionary monograph on Tibet came to my mind, Miss Taylor exerted herself so kindly and willingly to help me in obtaining information that at length I ventured to ask her whether she would trust me with her own contribution to the subject; in other words, whether I might have a look at the diary. In due time it arrived, and very odoriferous of Tibet, being packed with butter, fox-skins and goatskins, dried mutton, yaks' tails, and jo.

I made haste to examine it, and soon saw it would be a slow and serious task deciphering those already half-obliterated hieroglyphics. It was done at last, however, by patient poring over each page in succession, a magnifying-glass in one hand and a pen in the other. There were a hundred and sixty-two closely written pages to be worked over in this way before it was possible to tell how much of the material might prove of use for publication.

The process of editing was only a little less difficult than that of transcription. There were odds and ends that could be pruned away at once, and redundant expressions which it was a comparatively simple matter to eliminate; but after this had been done there remained the bulk of the narrative in a form hardly suitable to put to press.

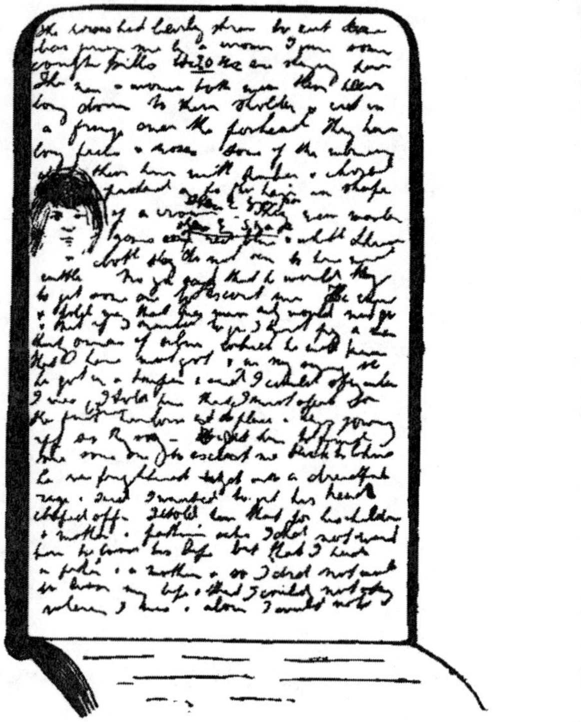

A PAGE OF THE DIARY.

There were slips of grammar, and crude forms of expression, most natural under the circumstances, which it was obviously a duty to set right, and in this respect I have dealt with the diary as I should wish my own unconsidered scribblings to be dealt with, were they placed in the compositors' hands. But no sentence has been touched that could be left, and practically the story as it is now published is the story as it was pencilled down under the freezing skies and over the bleak passes of wild Tibet.

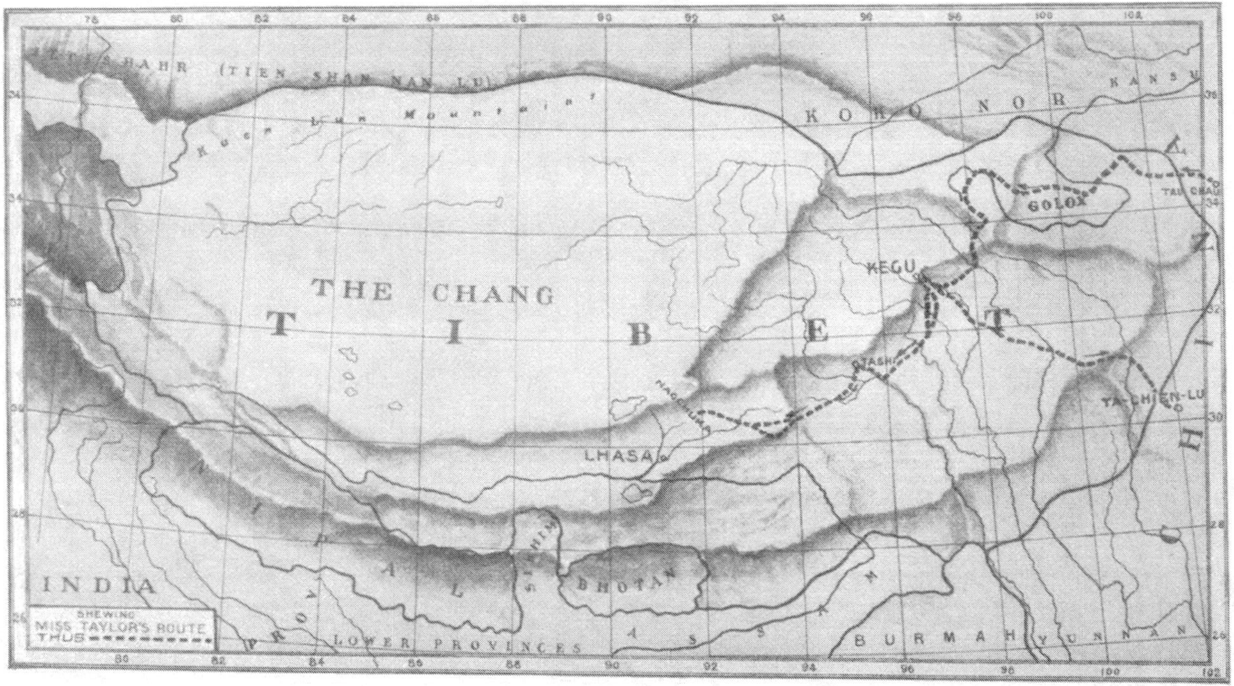

MAP OF TIBET.
Showing Miss Taylor's journey from Tau-chau to Ta-chien-lu.

Part II

Diary of
Miss Taylor's Journey
(FROM TAU-CHAU TO TA-CHIEN-LU)
Through Tibet.

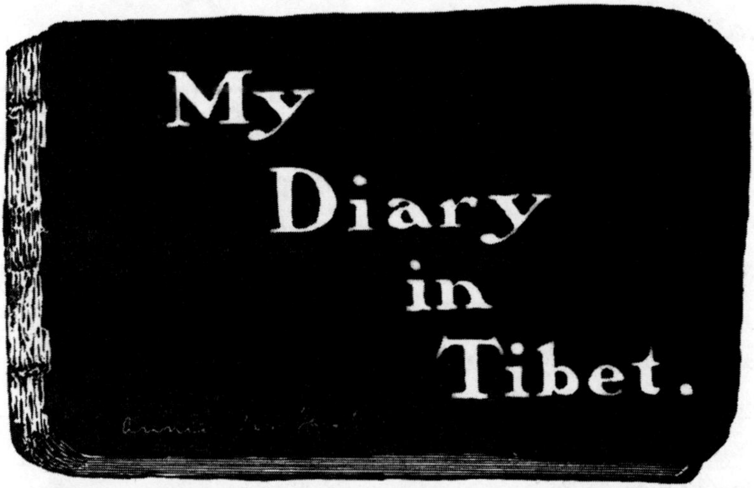

The surface of the book is of black glossy cloth; the edges of the leaves dirty, once red; the binding the worse for wear, bits of the black gone, and the stitching of the back showing underneath.

CHAPTER I

THE FIRST STAGES

The Start.—Stealing out of China.—Pursued.—Fight with Dogs. —Turned Back by a River.—Attacked by Brigands.—Flight Through the Waters.—Shelter at Last.—Black-Tent Hospitality.—A Black-Tent City.

SEPTEMBER 2, 1892.—The money having arrived yesterday, I was busy writing letters and thinking of all the things to put together for the journey. As we were to start at daybreak, we did not get much sleep. Pontso appeared at twelve o'clock, and then, when told it was too early, came about every hour to know the time.

We got up before daybreak and had some coffee.

Then prepared to start. The things left for us to carry were rather heavy; but as soon as the inner gate of the city was open we crept out of the house without waking the landlord's family, and made for the outer gate. It was closed. There was some difficulty in opening the lock, and we had to wait a few minutes; but no questions were asked about us from the guard's house.

We found our servant, Leucotze, with the horses, waiting outside the city, round a corner of the wall, dressed in Tibetan clothes. He led the way, we following. It being early, few saw us. We had to pass a gate, on a hill that separates China from Tibet, where custom dues are levied. We greatly feared the soldiers there would forbid us to pass. I went first. They asked the servants where I was going. They gave the name of some place or other. The man in charge said, "What is she going there for?" They said, "*Long chu la.*"

Once in, we hurried on. There were three or four Tibetan villages to pass, and then we had to climb a steep mountain. At the top we rested and put on Tibetan dress. Descending to the bottom on the other side, we found numerous villages. The harvest was ripe, and the people were busy getting it in. They use yaks to carry the corn home, and stack it on bars of wood to keep it dry. Only half the ground is sown each year, the other half being

A CHINESE CITY GATE.

KA GUMPA.
Overlooking Yatung.

ploughed three or four times to expose the soil to the sun and rain. The men, women, and children all wore sheepskins. They were too busy to take much notice of me.

We passed by Che ma yan ka Gumpa, situated on a hillside, opposite fields of corn in a very fruitful valley. Then through some more villages, after which we turned off the road into a dell, where we found the rest of our party, including Noga and his wife Erminie, a Lhasa woman. They had left the city the night before, going up some secret pass to evade the gates, of which there are three.

The tents were already pitched, and they soon put up my travelling-bed. I was very stiff. They made tea, and soon boiled some mutton, which we ate with our fingers and drank the broth. Leucotze and Nobgey had to go back to fetch the bride of the latter. They were to return at dark, but did not. The Lhasa woman had to alter the style of her hair, and, while doing it, told me that she was never well unless she had lice in her hair and on her clothes, and asked me the reason why—which I could not tell her. Pontso then said that many people in Tibet have riches when they have lice, but that their money all goes when they kill the lice. Went to bed at dusk.

September 3.—It rained fast in the night. Our companions did not turn up. I found some splendid mushrooms this morning, and, the grass being very good, we were not sorry to stay another day. Sorted our things, and made them into more convenient bundles for travelling. After this I was [illegible] I had a bad headache, Tibetan food and my digestive apparatus not being accustomed to each other. They will get on better on further acquaintance.

At dusk the man and his lady-love made their appearance. They had been hiding in the neighborhood since noon. She was decked with no end of jewelry. We started, and it soon got dark. Our way lay over a high mountain, which in the daytime is patrolled by robbers. We hoped to give them the slip by travelling at night. The descent was very difficult. The others walked, but I rode. We could not see the track, and all the horses had to be led. Lam ma Gumpa and La ra la were passed. It was so dark in the valley that we had to call out to one another.

At a bridge, called Don re ko, we met a wild man who asked where we were going. He seemed to take great notice of us. Very frightened, we crept on in the dark, over mountains and through valleys, and day was just breaking when our guide, Noga, told me to go in front of him, as some men were coming. I had no sooner done so than a stampede took place, and the lovers and Leucotze bolted. In the meantime, our pack-horses had all scattered. Pontso, Erminie, and I were left alone. We went after our baggage, and found one horse had thrown his load. It seems that the woman was the wife of another man, from whom she had run away to join Nobgey. Her husband was one of the pursuers. The couple were soon caught and brought back. We had

A TIBETAN VALLEY.

reached a place called Naen Pen. Nobgey was quite crestfallen, for the husband had told him that he would have his ears cut off. Our guide went to try to make peace. The pursuers wanted us to stop, and were very noisy, following us along. At last, Noga succeeded in coming to terms with them, but Nobgey had to lose a horse, and I a bag full of things. We hurried on for fear of further trouble.

At Ma re Gumpa we rested for tea, and just before dark came to Maz cha. Here the people put us up for the night in a funny little house built into the side of a hill. Our host and two friends promised to come with us next day as guides. The road is notorious for robbers.

September 5.—We started at daybreak, after tea and bread. The guides were waiting outside the village, all mounted, and armed with guns and swords. They led us a little distance, and then dispersed to pick raspberries on the slope of the hill! Noga joined them, and brought me back some. They lingered for other sport by large pools and hollows in the mountain-side. We climbed the mountain and met only two robbers; one had a gun and the other a long lance.

From Len ten la we descended to the drogpa country. Our guard here left us. We encamped for the midday meal near some shepherds at San de ku. Noga bargained with a lama for a sheep, and the lama himself drove it in. Noga killed it, telling the lama to keep his eyes away while the soul migrated. This he did by turning his back; but, when it was killed, he quite enjoyed helping to skin and dress it. It was getting late, so we had to start. While we were passing the black tents of the shepherds, about fifty great dogs came out and attacked us. They were driven off, but the horses were much frightened. Those of Pontso and Noga rushed past me riderless, and were caught only with a great deal of trouble. One horse kicked off its load, and then lay down in the stream.

It was nearly dark when we reached She tsong Gumpa. They gave us a big room in the Gr but we were all smoked out as soon as the fire was lighted. We cooked the liver of the sheep for supper, but had to eat it without bread, as the big bag of bread had been lost or stolen during the day. Our servant busied himself making sausages.

September 6.—We have to halt for a day, the Tao ho (or Le chu, as the river is called in Tibetan) being in flood. It is too swollen for us to cross. The ferry-boat has been swept away and smashed, also a bridge which they had tried to throw over instead. We cannot go by the Dru wa la, as the lamas here are at enmity with the people that live there, and will not give us an escort.

In the afternoon we heard a scuffle in the courtyard of the chief lama, our host. Six robbers had carried off two horses, and the owners were going after them. Later on they returned, bringing the horses, the robbers having abandoned them on being pursued.

September 7.—We started at dawn, and tried to

cross the river at several places. But not a man or a horse, even without its saddle, could do it. So it was no use for our loaded ones to try. It was quite exciting to watch the lama struggling with the water as he tried in vain to cross. There was nothing for it but to wait a day or two, or else go through the robber country. We decided to do the latter, and sent for two extra men as escort, making five in all.

It was a weary march up the mountain, and we halted at one o'clock in a glen just below the pass. Here we had tea, and let the horses graze. At four we started again, three of the men going in front and two behind. All went well until dusk. We were following the river, which here winds across a plain, with hills on our right. Noga and the lama, who were riding ahead, returned, and made signs to hasten us on. We came as quickly as we could, driving on the horses with the loads. All got their guns ready, for the brigands had been sighted, sitting on a plateau, a little distance off. When they saw us, they jumped on their horses, for they had been drinking tea, and the lama, with three others, gave a shout and rushed towards them. Leucotze was behind, with two of the loads. Erminie, Pontso, and I drove on the rest, and tried to get past before the firing began. I counted the robbers. There were eight of them, while on our side were only five fighting men, but in the dusk we must have seemed a host.

One of the five had to go forward with us to show us the way, leaving four to fight. The firing commenced, and frightened the animals, so we had not much trouble in hurrying them on. We drove them as fast as we could, praying as we went. Darkness set in, and we could still hear the firing. After a while we stopped, fancying we heard Leucotze coming up behind. He brought the two missing beasts of burden, and also Noga's horse. We came to a river. It was very deep, but there was not much time to think. We went through it, driving the horses before us. The water came half-way up our legs. Then we hurried on. It began to rain, but we dared not stop to put on our wraps. Wet as we were, we still kept going on, till at last, to our great relief, Noga overtook us. He said the firing had ceased, and that none of them were hurt, but that three of the escort had stayed behind to prevent the robbers' giving chase. By this time, the rain was pouring in torrents. We struggled forward as best we could, with wet clothes and feet, in the cold mountain air. At one place the river had to be crossed again, and the strong current nearly carried away one of the horses with its load. It was past midnight when we reached a large encampment of black tents.

There were about two hundred in all, and they belonged to the relatives of the lama. The dogs were troublesome, but we soon put our own tents up, and, taking off our wet clothes, went to rest. The people gave us some tea, mixed with butter and barley-flour, and it did seem so good, being hot.

September 8.—We were up at sunrise. An old woman invited me into her tent. Their tents are from five to six feet high, raised in the centre, and about twenty feet long by eighteen broad. In the interior the boxes are always all on one side, and they build up a stove of mud, and have many iron or copper pans. The old woman, while she talked with me, busily pulled a string which turned a large praying-wheel, so as to lose no time. She first gave me some milk, and then asked me to feel the pulse of some one who was ill.

We secured twelve men to escort us on, some going in front, some behind, and others at our sides, flourishing their long spears and guns. We exchanged a horse for one of theirs. Noga's horse tried to throw Leucotze, going down on its knees and then rearing up. At midday we came to another encampment of Tibetans and Mongols, and there set up our tents. They invited us into one of their own to drink tea, and we went. There is a Chinaman here, and also a "living Buddha" from

TIBETAN NOMADS ON THE CHANG.

TIBETAN GUIDES.

Laberlong. I should think there are quite a thousand tents in sight, black and white. These, with the yaks, sheep, and horses, look picturesque.

CHAPTER II

EIGHTEEN DAYS IN A MONGOL ENCAMPMENT

On the Move Again.—Siberian Mongols.—Second Attack by Brigands.—Bloodshed.—Goods all Stolen.—Life in a Mongol Encampment.—Nobgey Returns.—Trouble with Noga.—A Friendly Lama.—Interior of Mongol Tent.—Storm.—Wolves.—Frightening out the Devil.—Yellow River Swollen and Impassable, Hence Forced to Wait.—Raids from the Camp.—A Mongol Tournament.—Noga Signs an Agreement.—Preparing to Start.

SEPTEMBER 9.—Started early and joined a company of Mongols. They had been to Siberia to sell their wool and buy barley-flour, etc. Their caravan consists of fifty yaks, all laden, as well as a few horses. Most of the men rode on horses, but some on yaks. They were nearly all armed, and, with our own escort of about twenty men, we made a brave show.

We stopped just for a short time at noon, and had tea near a stream, then pushed on quickly, the country being infested with brigands. Now and then the escort would scatter to see whether any were hiding behind the hills. We saw numbers of deer and other animals, and the soldiers amused themselves by hunting a fine wild goat.

We were going along quietly enough, when, all of

a sudden, two of those in front came galloping back to say the robbers were upon us. We looked up, and saw numbers of them coming over the crest of the hill, all armed and many of them leading an extra horse. We went back a little, but were shut up in a hollow surrounded by hills. Ten of our men advanced to meet the robbers, but, on seeing their numbers, returned. We kept close to the yaks, looking to see which way to go. By this time robbers were seen on the tops of the hills all round, and they were closing in upon us. There was nothing to do but to stand still. Then they fired on us from all sides. Men and horses fell down dead or wounded. Bullets were flying. There was hardly a sound to be heard except the guns and the cries of fear from the Lhasa women. The firing was so hot that one of the lamas asked Noga to go and tell them we would surrender. He went towards them, making peaceful signs; but as soon as he got near they took hold of his horse, and, after a scuffle, captured his gun and sword. Erminie shrieked when she saw her husband unhorsed, thinking he was killed. The Mongols shouted that they surrendered, and the brigands rushed to take the yaks. Erminie, Pontso, Nobgey, and I ran towards a gorge in the mountains, which the lama pointed out, telling us to be quick, and crying out to the robbers that we were women.

We did not know whether they would come after us or not. Two Mongols, badly wounded, were galloping away in front of us, and we followed them. When we got over the crest of the hill, Nobgey went back to see how it fared with the rest. Leucotze, with two of the pack-horses, was surrounded by the robbers, and Nobgey brought us word that he feared they had killed him. Nothing could be seen of Noga.

We then went on again in the track of the wounded men. Large herds of deer started at our flight, and soon we lost all signs of the path. Finally, an encampment came in sight, and we were most thankful to reach it. The people at first received us coldly; but on hearing that we were with the party attacked they were most kind, bringing us tea and barley-flour, and helping to unload the horses. Numbers of armed men were already galloping from all sides to the scene of the fight, for our Mongol companions belong to this encampment. They gave us plenty of jo (yak-dung) to make a fire, and also some tea, and lent us a large pan to make it in. We put our things together as best we could, and with the felt mats that covered the loads I made a bed and lay down to rest. The others were sitting by the fire wrapped in their fur cloaks. Nobgey again returned to get news of our missing ones.

September 10.—At daybreak all was astir, and a man brought us word that our comrades were well and most of the loads had been saved. But about midday they appeared *without* the loads. The horses had been captured as well as the goods, and only two bags of barley-flour were saved. Leucotze was guarding the horses, but two robbers with drawn swords had compelled him to dismount, and had taken possession of the loads. All my clothes and the camp-bed and my bedding were gone. Noga had a scar on his neck, which he said was made by a stroke from the back of a sword, whether by mistake or of purpose we cannot tell; but I thank God for giving me the lives of those with me. One man was killed on the spot, and ten others were wounded. Our escort all fled, leaving the Mongols with the yaks. Seven horses were killed, and one yak; and the principal man of the Mongols was taken prisoner.

The brigands proved too strong for those who went out from the encampment on hearing the shots. There are said to be two hundred of them.

Noga has friends in the encampment; so we moved to where they were, they lending us a black tent and a cooking-pan, as we had now none of our own. They also made us a present of a sheep, which Leucotze set to work to kill and dress. Noga had a long talk with the people, to whom he seems to be well known. They are all bandits, and go out in companies to attack unwary travellers; so I think he must have been a robber, too. He has decided to pay a visit to the camp of our assailants, as he knows one of their chiefs, and see whether he can recover some of the stolen goods.

September 11.—Noga asked for something to offer the chief, and I went to the box in which articles for presentation had been put, but found that

OFFERING THE KHATA.

he had stolen most of them before starting from China, and left them in his house. He admitted having done this, and did not seem at all ashamed. About ten o'clock he went off with some others, taking Leucotze with him. He was angry and rude because I would not let Pontso go as well. We have to settle down for some time now in our tent. It is made of yak's hair, not very closely woven, so that when it rains the water comes in.

September 12.—Most of our neighbors returned to-day, as they heard that a gang of marauders was in the neighborhood and they feared for their flocks.

September 13.—A number of the men, about one hundred, went out to look for the gang this evening.

September 14.—At daybreak the scouts returned,

having been unsuccessful in tracing the gang. In the afternoon eight men, fully armed, passed by, leading three horses. We heard they had taken them from travellers. Stealing and highway robbery are considered very brave and right in this part of the world.

The lama who told us to flee, and told the robbers we were women, has been two or three times to see us. Nobgey has decided to go back to China. He has lost another of his horses, and his silver, and nearly all his goods; and, as there are some lamas going to Laberlong, he will go with them. Erminie is very much put out about it, and wants him to stay until her husband returns; but he will not do so. She got the lama to talk to him, but without success. He says that without the other woman he has no desire to go to Lhasa. They made great fun of him, but he stuck to his determination. He has exchanged his barley-flour for butter, and his other goods for leather; and he hopes to do some business.

September 15.—Nobgey left us at daybreak, taking a letter from me. Two men are sitting outside the chief's tent, in irons, for stealing. I have a number of patients to see daily, and they bring me butter, cheese, and milk. One has promised me a sheep. The people here all have large flocks of sheep, and herds of yaks and horses, which they take out to graze in the morning, bringing them back at night. The women churn, and make cheese of the buttermilk daily, also curds of the milk, which they call *sho.* I have quite a number of friends here. Pontso looks after the horses. We are daily expecting the arrival of Noga. His wife has a dream at night, and says he will come; but he does not turn up.

September 17.—In the evening the lama paid us a visit. He said that our stars were good, and that by means of dice the gods had told him Noga would arrive to-day; and therefore he had come expecting to see him. After we had lain down for the night, and it was raining fast, we heard a noise, the dogs barked, and then Noga and Leucotze appeared. Noga has recovered three of the horses, my bed, and a few

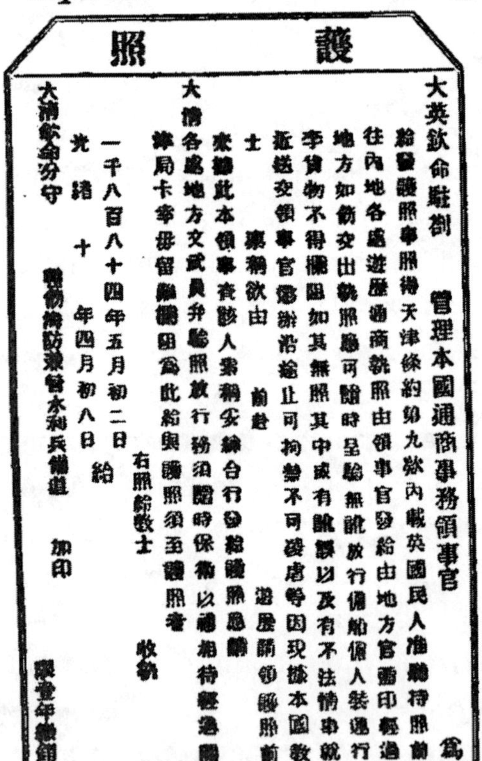

A CHINESE PASSPORT.

of my clothes, and also a little of my bedding, but *all* his own things, though none of Pontso's. He had pretended to be a servant of Ser Gon Lama Hu Tu Tuk of Cho Per Che, a great man in these parts. He is a general to whom the emperor of China has given a lot of land. The people expect that he will some day be king of Tibet. He says that in a former birth he was once emperor of China, and before that a big European chief. Noga got an old passport of his from one of his servants, and he trades on that. I found that he was wearing one of my flannel jackets.

September 18.—I asked Noga in the morning to give me the jacket, as Pontso and I had no more clothing, and charged him with taking the two fur gowns. He got into a rage; and, coming over to where I was lying down, attempted to strike me. Pontso and the servant prevented him; and I ran out, going into one of the Mongol tents for refuge. The people were most kind, giving me milk to drink. I sent for the lama to help me. He came and spoke to Noga, and another of the Mongols took my part. They put up my tent for me, and I said that I must return to Tau-chau, as I could not go on with such a man. All day long they talked, but it was to no purpose. Noga quarrelled with the lama. The lama was most kind.

September 19.—Pontso kept guard over me. The

Mongols had to go for some ceremony to a distant hill. Noga sent his servant to pull down my tent; but I cried out, and he went away, as he feared the people. In the evening the men returned, and they spoke to Noga. He says that he wants wages, but is not my servant. They talked until quite late.

September 20.—Pontso thinks that we shall be able to go on, that Noga will repent. He has gone to-day with some Mongols to another encampment to see whether he can get two horses lent him. The Mongols here all take my part. The Lord is good; I will not fear what man shall do unto me. The Mongol tents are very comfortable. The sides are of trellis-work covered with felt, and the top is also covered with white felt, a hole being left in the middle for the smoke to go out; but at night that is covered over. Their fireplaces are strong, well raised, and made of clay.

The tents are round, and have a small wooden door. They are easily taken down and put up. There is plenty of standing-room in them. The man that promised me a sheep gave it to-day. It is a very fine fat one, and we have all been busy helping to cut it up.

September 21.—In the afternoon a dreadful storm of snow and wind sprung up. I held the posts of my tent to keep it from being blown down. Erminie and Leucotze had a quarrel. He says that he

PONTSO.

TAKING TEA IN TIBETAN STYLE.

In the centre is Miss Taylor; at the left is Pontso, holding a leather bag of barley-flour; on the right is his wife, holding the teapot; the three wooden bowls are the teacups. At the extreme right is a bamboo churn; in front of it, goatskin bellows with an iron funnel; and in the centre of the picture, in front, are leather bags for tea, butter, etc.

CHURNING TEA.

TIBETAN WOMEN
DANCERS.

THE DEVIL DANCE.

LAMAS MASKED FOR THEIR
RELIGIOUS PANTOMIME
OR DEVIL DRAMA.

will not go on to Lhasa unless I go. Pontso says that this is an answer to his prayers. I have not been at all well, and am able to take only milk; but the Mongols are most kind. In the height of the storm one of them came to see whether he could do anything for me, and put some hot ashes in my foot-warmer. At night there was a great row, and Noga returned to the settlement.

September 22.—Our guide has got one horse lent him, but he has to pay twelve taels for the other as deposit. He wanted me to pay this for him. He apologized for what he did, and promised to behave in the future. I would not listen for a long time, but at last let him have five taels. A letter of agreement between us is to be written.

This afternoon a large pack of gray wolves trotted along the hills. The Mongols feared these would attack their sheep, but they passed on. Yesterday there were several large deer with long black horns. The people said that some Chinese merchants had killed one lately, and that is the reason there is so much rain now.

September 23.—This morning a lama with feathers in his hair, and wearing a mask, was driving away some of the yaks; they were supposed to be bewitched, and he was frightening the devil out of them. All the people followed him, and consulted him about their cattle.

The Yellow River is swollen, so we cannot go on for the present. The tent freezes at night, and is a sheet of ice. But in the day the weather is warm and bright. Late in the afternoon some men came galloping to the encampment; and instantly all the camp was in motion, the horses being driven in and saddled, and the guns and spears got out, and the men hasting to mount. Some robbers had come to the farther end of the camp and stolen some horses, and they were bound to pursue them. One of our horses was at that end, and so it, too, may be amongst those stolen.

September 24.—We hear that eight horses were stolen. Those in pursuit have not yet returned. The father of Ar Gu Qua Main, the one who is so kind to me, told me with evident pride that the best horse his son has was taken from these very men, who have now retaliated by taking some of theirs. The old men, the boys, and the women look after the cattle, while the others are away fighting. They seem much to enjoy their raids on other encampments.

September 25.—Late last night the Mongols returned, not having come up with the horse-stealers. In the morning there was a military tournament in which all the fighting men took part on horseback, fully armed. Most of the young ladies of the encampment went to see the sight, mounted on yaks, some of them with a child behind. One of the sports was to fire at a given spot while going at full gallop. It was a very pretty sight.

Pontso is in low spirits, and will not go on unless a good agreement is written.

September 26.—This morning we have at last got an agreement written out, and Noga and Pontso went to the chief to get it signed; but he is waiting for the lama to be present. Our camp is all in motion. We hope to start to-morrow. May the Lord bless us on our way and preserve us from all danger!

September 27.—When we got up, it was raining fast; but we made preparations for starting. Ar Gu Qua Main had said he was not going; but Noga beat his wife last night, and this gave me a pretext for asking his escort; and after some persuasion he consented. The chief stamped the agreement, and gave us a present of butter and cheese. The lama Am Jo also came to say good-by. By the time we were ready to start the storm had ceased. We passed large herds of deer, and then came to the Yellow River, which runs between steep banks. Encamped by the river. Beautiful wild flowers. It rained fast in the evening. I pitied the poor men having to sleep out in the wet, and lent them some covering. Ar Gu Qua Main and Pontso shared the tent with me.

CHAPTER III

WITH THE GOLOK TRIBE IN THE LOOP OF THE YELLOW RIVER

Crossing the River.—Entering the Land of the Golok.—Tough Marches.—Lost in the Snow.—A friendly Chinaman.—Blue Lake Guides.—More Snow.—Taken for Robbers.—Crossing the Yellow River Again.—A Terrible Time.

SEPTEMBER 28.—In the morning we moved to the spot we had to cross (*ma chu*). Four bullock-skins were blown out and planks lashed over and around them. Two ferrymen, with their clothes tied up in a sheepskin, held the reins of two horses, lay flat on the water, and so towed us across. Two more men floated behind. Erminie, Pontso, and I crossed first. It took a long time to ferry us all. The horses were the most troublesome, three of them being carried down the stream and having to be brought up by land and made to try again. One man would lead in three or four horses by cords, but have to let some of them go in mid-stream. It was four o'clock in the afternoon before we were safely on the other side. The ferrymen felt the cold very much. They each got twenty-two feet of red cotton cloth, about a foot wide, for taking us over. Red cotton cloth is the currency in this part of the world.

September 29.—Up before daybreak. At midday entered the Golok country among the snow-topped mountains.

September 30.—Crossed three mountains. The country here is all hills and swamps. The Golok men and women are much shorter than the Mongols. No grass on the tops of the mountains—all bare rock. Iron colors the water. We climbed through the snow-clouds. Hired two men to escort us for three days at two pieces of cloth each, each piece forty feet long.

October 1.—Crossed the Ko Chu River and passed a number of black-tent encampments; the road rises gently between the mountains. Got into a bad snowstorm, the wind driving it in our faces. Saw a number of birds with long black legs and necks, and gray bodies.

October 2.—Snowed all night and still snowing when we started. Travelled all day in a violent snowstorm. Had difficulty in keeping the road, often losing it. Arrived late, and quite done up, at a large black-tent encampment, Hun ku ma re mong. They say the mountains here are called Tsong ge mong. Leucotze not at all well.

October 3.—We are resting here, for Leucotze is ill. The Yellow River, which we have to cross again, is said to be impassable. A Chinese merchant from Chen Tu Schuen is here. He is only seventeen, and seems quite pleased to meet some of his countrymen.

October 4.—Leucotze a little better. Snowed all last night, but cleared up this afternoon. We were not able to go on.

October 5, 6, 7.—Still here, the waters being too high to attempt a crossing. Heavy snow and very cold. The Chinese youth gave me a foxskin dress. He is returning to Chen Tu in a day or two. He hires yaks to carry his goods. He is taking back wool. It takes him about a month to get to Chen Tu from here.

The men here wear an earring like a rat's tail in one of their ears. They are big, fat men. They are most of them well-to-do, having a lot of cattle. They wear cotton or cloth from Lhasa over their sheepskin gowns. The chief gave us a sheep. This was killed the last day, as well as one we got in exchange.

October 8.—Started again. Have two men to escort us. They belong to the Blue Lake, but are living in Golok. One is a lama, but he is also a hatter, for he made my foxskin cap for me. They are both big, fine men. There is snow on the ground, and it is very cold, a piercing wind. Met numbers of people with their yaks and goods going

MISS TAYLOR IN TIBETAN DRESS.
The cap is of fox-skin, made for her in the Mongol encampment.

down to the warmer parts. The snow has set in. Reached the Drun chu har ma Road, and stayed at Tan ka yong.

October 9.—Got up before daybreak—very cold. White snow and blue sky all that is to be seen. On the top of the mountains our guide tried to kill a deer, but missed it. Encamped by a stream. No wood or jo to be got, and only a little wood with us; so nothing but tea after a hard day.

October 10.—Went all day through the snow, the ground being very uneven and hard for the horses. The sun is hot in the middle of the day, and the glare very trying. Pontso was quite ill with it. Two fine hares ran away from quite near us. Rat tracks all over the snow. After resting we noticed two men driving their loads. Our escort went to see who they were. They were driving the loads at a great rate. They took us for robbers. They were Tibetan merchants from So pa ba nak going to Amjore. Late in the afternoon we descended from the mountains into a plain. We settled for the night by a river E chu, running into the Yellow River.

October 11.—Started before daybreak. Had gone some way when men were sighted. Our guide and one of the escort went on to see who they were. Had first got their guns ready. They were only some Tibetans, with yaks, going to fetch wood from

Sha Toong. We reached the Yellow River at midday and crossed the first half, it being here divided by some hills, and then rested for tea, the guides and escort going on to the other half to try it. The bed of the river is most uneven, and this makes it difficult to cross. We passed a number of horseshoe walls, which must be used to pitch tents in during the summer.

The river is quite impassable, so they say; but we are waiting until to-morrow to see if it will be lower in the morning. The Lord can do this for me. My eyes are unto Him who made a passage in the Red Sea for the children of Israel. One of our escort rode my horse to try to get over, but the horse threw him and broke his gun.

October 12.—Our escort crossed the river, the water coming up to the horses' heads. Pontso said that only their ears were visible. The river here divides into three streams, the furthest one being the most difficult to cross. There is gold in the river, and on the mountains; the Chinese come for it in the summer.

Some ducks flew by from over the river and a swarm of teal making for the south. We can hear dogs barking on the other side, so think that men must be near. Our escort have gone to find some one to lead us over. This is a very dangerous place for brigands; they attack the caravans at night.

Pontso is to help in case we are attacked, but I do not think he will be of much use.

October 13.—We got ready to move early in the morning, but there were no signs of our escort. Two hunters were sighted going with dogs after deer. Our guide asked them to show us the crossing-place. They said they would, but wanted ten pieces of cloth; so it was no use. After midday we started, hoping to meet the escort. We went down-stream, where the hunters had come from, and hoped to see their horses' tracks in the sand. When we had gone some way, one of our escort turned up dripping wet. He had been nearly carried away while crossing. He told us the old lama had attempted to cross, but had to return, and that the chief on the other side of the river would send two men to show us the way next day. Encamped for the night where we were, Erminie crying at prospect of crossing the river.

October 14.—Early in the morning Pontso came, and said that twenty men all on horseback were coming, and feared they were robbers; so I got up at once. The rest were talking about what to do. When the mist cleared away, the robbers proved to be wild horses feeding in the distance! Later on, we sighted two men on the other side of the river. They had come to show us the way. We made for the place, and found they had brought two yaks to help carry the goods over. After a few attempts the men succeeded in getting over to us, but could not bring the yaks, as the waters were too deep.

While they drank tea, we got ready to cross, taking off our boots and hooking up our gowns. We looked fine frights. At last, one of the men started; I followed; then Pontso, leading a pack-horse; then Noga, leading his wife's mount; and then the other man with a pack-horse, and last of all Leucotze, who had tied a rope to the dog and was leading it along.

The horses soon got out of their depth and had to swim. It was startling to see the one in front disappear, all except its tail, and then to feel mine do likewise. Erminie gave a scream, the girth of her saddle having broken. Leucotze came to her help, and held her on the horse. There were four streams. This was the second. The next two were not so bad, but the current was very swift. All reached the other side safely, but Leucotze in his usual style had carefully led the rope over without the dog!

We took off our wet things, feeling very cold. The snow lay thick on the ground. Noga, Leucotze, and one of the men had to cross again to fetch the other loads. All came safely, the dog of his own accord.

Although the encampment was near, it was late

when we reached it. We could not put ours near the tent of the chief, as his daughter had been gored by a yak and was lying dangerously ill. It was feared that strangers, coming from a distance, might bring ill luck, and she might die. The place is Sha way ma, and the chief is a woman, her name Wa Chu Bu Mu. Her husband was chief till he died.

CHAPTER IV

SQUABBLES, SICKNESS, AND DEATH

Halt.—Noga Beats His Wife.—The Chieftainess.—An English Traveller.—Waiting for a Pair of Boots.—Start Again.—Leucotze Ill.—Halt.—Death of Leucotze.—Start Again.—Wild Horses Make a Path Through the Snow.—The Dog Missing.—Glare of the Snow.—Yak Skulls and Eagles.—Miss Taylor too Ill to go On.—Noga Resolves to Desert.—The White Face Betrays Itself.—Pontso Afraid.—The First House Seen for Two Months.

OCTOBER 15.—We are staying here for a day or two. Noga has been trying to exchange some of our lean horses for fat ones, but has not yet succeeded.

This evening I heard Noga and his wife quarrelling, and then a scuffle. I went to see what it was, and found him dragging her by the hair and kicking at her, and Pontso trying to prevent him. I got between them, and after a while he released her. I told her to go to my tent. I had a long talk with him, and he promised not to beat her again. She has been finding fault with Leucotze, who says that he will go no further than the next stage; and this frightened Noga, and he blamed his wife for it. She blamed him, and then he pinched her cheek, Tibetan fashion. I asked him whether he was not ashamed to blame her when he himself had been scolding Leucotze all the time. Finally, I got her to return to her tent, and all seemed right; but after I had gone to bed she came back again in tears, her husband having been thumping her; and in a little while he followed with his horsewhip. I told her to get behind my bed, and then seized hold of the whip, and screamed, which frightened him. I told him he must go out of my tent. Pontso with his blanket wrapped round him tried to hold him; but, being so little a man and Noga tall, it was not much use. Erminie got behind me, and I told him that he had promised not to quarrel, and that if this went on we could not go to Lhasa. Pontso told him that he would make me ill, as I was shivering all over with the cold. He at last went away, and Erminie returned, leaving us in peace.

October 16.—We have bought a fine sheep for twenty feet of cloth, and every one is busy dressing it. Noga went to pay his respects to the chieftainess. She said that two hundred robbers or soldiers had gone on the road we are going. They come from Ser La, and are going to fight some other clan at Sa Ge Kar. She fears that we may meet them, and that if we do they will steal our horses and goods; but she says that the two men who will be our escort will speak to them, and unless they kill them there will not be any danger. The snow on the road is very deep. Just lately, six men trying to cross lost two of their yaks.

The women here wear their hair in numbers of little plaits. Some do nothing to their hair at all. They have big noses. They wear no earrings or jewelry, but they have lots of cattle. Our lady chief has six hundred yak, and a chief further up, they say, has two thousand cattle.

October 17.—We moved to-day to a place near the tent of the chieftainess. She came and paid us a visit. She is not very old, and she is very pleasant. She brought me some milk. Noga was rude to me, but afterwards apologized. The chief wants a pair of Chinese leather boots for her son, a boy of about eleven; and, as I cannot wear mine, I am letting her have them. She is getting a warm pair of boots made for me. They say that an Englishman came here about three years ago. He rode one horse, and on another carried iron boxes. He paid for everything in silver, so must be very rich. He had a very big passport written in Chinese, and a copy of it in Tibetan. This is the emperor of China's letter. The people here wanted to see what was in the boxes, but feared; for they said if the boxes were broken open soldiers would come out. They said he slept at night with one cloth over his head, and another over his feet. They say also that six persons passed this way, amongst them one woman, and that none of the chiefs would let them pitch their camp on their ground. They also say that there is an Englishman selling and giving away books at Sining.

October 18.—My boots are not finished; so we must wait another day. The chieftainess came to pay me a special visit in my own tent. The cloth attached to her hair is decked with coral and large pieces of amber.

October 19.—Started again. Passed a herd of about thirty wild horses. The two men escorting us say that they know I am English, for they have seen English people. All fear they will spread the report in advance; and Noga and Pontso are therefore in a very bad humor. We exchanged one of our sick horses for a smaller one and a piece of cloth and some foxskins. Wolves howling at night; Pontso says this is a bad sign.

October 20.—We were ready to start early, but Leucotze complained of being ill, and for a long time could not be persuaded to get up, saying he would rather be left behind. We travelled only two hours, and then were obliged to stop, as Leucotze was really ill. One of the escort told Noga there are five hundred soldiers ahead, and that they stole all the things of some Chinese merchants who preceded us; and he advised us not to continue our journey. I am for going on, but the others want to return. The Lord will open up the way somehow. I gave Leucotze beef tea and brandy, and let him sleep in my tent. The sickness soon ceased, but he complained of great pain in his chest; his breathing was very laborious, and his pulse could not be felt.

October 21.—Leucotze had a very bad night. I gave him chlorodyne in large doses; but he could not sleep, and kept on saying, "*Tong se le-az.*" In the night I got some snow for him. The cold was most bitter, everything freezing. I took hold of the handle of my knife, and it stuck to my fingers, taking the skin off.

The escort said they would not wait; so we tried to get Leucotze up, but it was no use; he was too ill to move. There seemed little hope of his getting better. Noga and Pontso washed him, in accordance with a Mohammedan custom, after which he got worse and worse, not being able to speak. Noga read to him out of the Koran, and Leucotze called upon Allah. About one o'clock he died. They had to wash his body again, and in some wet soil dug a grave about a foot deep, the two men that escorted us helping. The place is called Per Go. The sun shone brightly, and the wind went down. I had given them the only piece of white cotton cloth I had, and so we buried him. I had tried to tell him the gospel at Tau Chau Zung, but he would not listen to it, saying that he was a Mohammedan. He was a big, strong-looking man, and wore a large sheepskin gown. The Master has called to account the strong, and left the weak to go on and claim Tibet in his name.

Noga read the Koran again at the head of the grave. He said that his soul would go to his home, and his mother would know. Leucotze's last word was "Allah!"

October 22.—We got up early and were soon on the way. Noga read from the Koran once more before we left. We had gone some distance when the escort started to hunt two foxes. They told us to go on; but we soon had to stop and wait for them, not knowing the way. We feared they had decamped, as their wages were paid in advance. These were the only terms they would come on. We waited patiently, and at last, to the joy of all, I caught sight of them coming. They had killed one of the foxes.

After this, we overtook a herd of eighteen wild horses making for the south. Going in front of us, one after another, they made a path in the deep snow. They seem to know what course to take in the drifts better than man. We also passed ten wild yak, fine-looking creatures, quite black. The sun and the snow again tried our eyes very much, in spite of the fact that we all wore native glasses, which are dark nets made of horsehair and edged with cloth. Our dog got lost going after the horses. He, like Leucotze, had come with us from Tau-chau, and now they are both left behind. May the Lord spare the rest of us to reach Darjiling!

October 23.—About midnight the dog made his appearance, having found us out. Saw numbers of wild horses. They are of drab color, and lighter underneath the body. They are slighter in build than the domestic horse.

Passed more wild yak. Noga tried to shoot one, but missed. Numbers of yak skulls lie along the road, and black eagles (with a few white feathers in the breast) use them to perch on, as there are no trees or bushes.

Travelling due south nearly all day. The sun in my eyes and the glare of the snow made me ill. I held the reins as long as I could, and then Pontso led my horse until I could ride no longer. I should have fallen off if he had not caught me. Noga came running back to see what was the matter. It was no use. I could not go on. Having with us some mixed sal-volatile and brandy, they gave it to me, and then Noga went off to stop the loads. When he returned, I was feeling a little better; so they lifted me again on the horse and led me to the encampment.

October 24.—I could not get up very early, feeling so weak, but thank God I am able to go on. We went all day down a valley, following a stream which in time became a river. Passed numbers of bowlders, the first I have seen on the road. Our escort's dog killed another fox, which they forthwith skinned. Saw a number of deer and a small kind of wild duck with black head and white body. Very tired. We encamped near some black tents at Ma mo ke. A lot of wild sheep were on the hills just above us. They are hard to kill, but their flesh is good. The name of the district is Sa Ge Kar Am Ne.

October 26.—The sun was well up before we started. I had reminded Noga that both the horses which he wants to sell are mine. He got into a temper, and began to call out that I was "an Englishwoman," to let the people hear. He pretended that Pontso was taking me to Lhasa, and not he. All day again through a valley by a river, going due south. This seems to be our bearing now.

October 27.—Got up before daybreak and started without making tea. Presently we overtook an encampment on the move. They were crossing the river Da Chu. There were numbers of yak, sheep, and horses. The bigger children were on horseback, with cross boards before and behind their saddles, while the little ones squatted in panniers on the yaks, and the babies were carried in the bosom.

Noga tried to get them to change one of our horses, but they refused. We saw some eagles eating a dead body which had been cut in pieces.

To-day we have entered the district of Da Chu, which is governed by the Umba at Sining. Noga and Erminie were thrown from their horses. We did not go as far as we intended, but pitched our tents near an encampment.

A young man who has been a servant to some chief at Lhasa resides here, and told us all the news. He says the war with the English is not over, but that they intend to carry it on next year. There are brigands prowling about; so he and another man sat up with Noga and Pontso most of the night. They made such a noise singing that I could not get to sleep.

October 28.—Ka Nor Ka Nr. It is snowing. We are waiting to try and change two of our horses. Noga told Pontso that he would not go with us beyond a monastery which we shall reach in two days. They say that some Chinamen from Sining live there. The Lord, who is sending me on this journey, will undertake for me. Noga is frightened because they make remarks about my white face and want to know who I am. All must be right with the ambassador of the Lord. I am his charge.

"Peace, perfect peace, our future all unknown;
Jesus we know, and he is on the throne."

Pontso is afraid to go on; so I have given him nearly all the silver I have, in case he may have to leave in a hurry; that is, if the Chinese mandarin stops me or there is trouble with the Tibetans.

October 29.—Started before sunrise. The ground is very stony and there are great rocks. The hills are covered with brushwood, and the black tents have walls of stone built round them. Late in the afternoon we came in sight of a temple, with a small village round its base,—the first house we had seen for nearly two months. Noga went on ahead and found out a Tibetan he knew, who let us have a sort of shed to put up in. The climate here is much milder than we have had since we left the Mongol settlement. The horses had barley straw to eat, brought by a woman to whom I had given medicine for her cough.

CHAPTER V

NOGA'S ASSAULT

Noga Again.—Crossing the Di Chu in Skin Boats.—Arrive at Ga La.—Host Penting.—Noga Threatens Betrayal.—Pontso Worships the Idols.—Crossing the Rab La.—Avoiding a Town by Moonlight.—Stopped by Officials.—An Anxious Moment.—Yaks Carrying Tea.—Making Tea with Ice.—Three Lamas Join the Party.—Bitter Wind.—Noga's Assault on Miss Taylor.—Chinese Merchants Protect Her.—The Matter Referred to the Chief.—Penting Offers to Kill Noga.—Pontso Runs Away.—The Chief Very Kind.—Noga States His Terms.

OCTOBER 30.—She E Gumpa. We are halting here. The men and women both wear their hair loose over the shoulders, and cut in a fringe across the forehead. Their faces and noses are long. Some of the women deck their hair with amber and coral in the shape of a crown. They wear woollen gowns of red, blue, and white Lhasa cloth. They do not seem to have many cattle.

Noga said he would try to get some others to take me on, but that I must pay each man thirty ounces of silver, which he well knew I had not got. Otherwise I could stay where I was. I said that, in that case, I should have to speak to the mandarin at a place which they say is a day's journey from here, and get him to find me some one to take me back to China. This frightened him. He fell into a dreadful rage, and said I wanted to get his head chopped off. I told him that I did not want him to lose his life, but that I did not want to lose my own life either, and that I could not stay where I was, nor could I go on or return alone; the only course left me was to get an escort from the mandarin in charge of the soldiers. He then demanded a certificate in Chinese, which he would get written, and I was to sign, threatening all kinds of things if I refused. I said I would give him one in English, that I could not give it in Chinese, and that if he got it written every one would know that I had not given it to him. He went on storming the greater part of the night, but I took no notice.

October 31.—In the morning Noga said we had better go on to Pa Tong, as we could not stay where we were. So we started. One man came with us on foot. The road lay through a narrow valley, with fields of barley stubble on each side of a stream. It was quite a treat to see some cultivated land again. There were numbers of small villages scattered here and there on the mountain-sides. The mountains are high, but only the tops are covered with snow, the lower parts being wooded, with great rocks. Altogether, the scenery is the most pleasing we have seen.

When we came in sight of the river Di Chu, our guide and Noga went on ahead to the monastery to see the chief. At the ferry we found a party of Tibetans crossing in relays. Their dogs attacked us fiercely, and Pontso had to use his sword to beat them off. The boats are made of yak-skins stretched tightly over wicker frames. They are light and easily carried. Men and their luggage are ferried across, but the yaks and horses have to swim. While we were waiting, a sand-storm sprung up, making it very disagreeable. The horses crossed first; all rushed into the river at once. Then Noga and Erminie, in the two boats, with a portion of the goods, and, last of all, Pontso and I, with the remainder.

It was getting late; so we pushed on at once. The road lay to the right, by the riverside, but it was very stony, and in places very steep. We had to climb the worst hill we have yet come to. On reaching the top we caught sight of a Tibetan house. Noga had gone on ahead and looked up some people he knew. They came out to meet us, and took us to their house. The name of the place is Ga La. The houses here are two or three stories high, being built into the side of the hill. We are on the second story. They gave us tea and barley-flour. They say the road from here is infested with brigands.

November 3.—Noga came to tell me he means to go on; that the cause of his frequent anger is only his littleness of heart, while mine is too big; that I do not take enough precaution; and that if I am not careful I shall not be able to reach Lhasa. He is trying to get our host to go with us.

November 4.—The name of our host is Penting. He is going with us. Both he and his wife are very friendly. They bring me milk and other things. We are staying here for a few days. It snowed all last night and part of to-day, so that it would not do to start just yet. The road, they say, is very bad this year. A number of the inhabitants came in to see me.

November 5.—The weather has cleared up. Our host gave us a sheep, which Noga killed. He is a Mohammedan, and eats only meat killed after their fashion.

November 6.—The weather is still bright. I hope we shall soon be on the road again. Noga says he will not go into Lhasa with me, but choose a roundabout way, and meet me somewhere on the other side. May the Lord preserve us from all his wickedness!

November 7.—Noga quarrelled with his wife, and she came to me in tears. He said he would tell the authorities at Lhasa that she had brought an Englishwoman there from China, and that they would give him a lot of money for the information, and punish her, while he would be safe, as he is Chinese. The Lord will take care of us, I do not fear.

November 8.—Pontso says that Noga wants Hu Tuk's letter or passport. I cannot give it to him, for that is the only thing he fears. If I showed it to the Chinese mandarin, he would lose his life. I fear for others, not for myself. I asked the Lord to make him forget about it and not ask me for it.

November 9.—Penting, his wife, and two children seem quite fond of me. He told me with tears in his eyes that he would so miss his little ones when he goes with us to Lhasa. He went to the temple, and Pontso went with him. I was much hurt, for Pontso worshipped the idols. He knows better, and I told him so. He seemed sorry. The Lord forgive him! Poor, weak Pontso, may strength be given him to stand!

We expect to start to-morrow. The road is in the hands of brigands, but the Lord will take care of us. I care not for anything else, so that our lives be spared.

November 10.—We left very early. The road lay up a terribly steep mountain over the pass Rab La. The mountains on this side of the river Dru Chu are all steep and high, with sharp edges. We got to a small village, and put up there for the night. It was snowing in our faces with a bitter wind. The people gave us straw for the horses to eat.

November 11.—Village Rab Da. We got up long before sunrise, and started in order to pass unnoticed by a large town. It was moonlight. We could see the town. It is called Ma Len Tza, and is the largest we have passed. There seem to be shops in it by the look. A little beyond we came to the monastery of Ke Gu, and on the other side of the hill on which it is built the Chinese mandarin who rules all this district lives.

Noga feared we might meet some of the officials, but no one saw us. We then crossed a high pass called Tso Sen La, overtaking a lot of yaks carrying tea sewed up in skins. We met Tibetans with more yaks. They were all fully armed. Then three men stopped us, and asked us where we were going. One was a small Chinese official with a gold button. It was an anxious moment.

My horse seems quite done up; he fell down at the pass, and was got up only with difficulty. The sun shone brightly, making the weather much warmer. We stopped for the night on the mountain-side a little way off the road.

November 12.—Up a long valley. Passed hundreds of deer. Noga tried to kill some, but did not succeed. My horse got so tired that I mounted a little white pony instead. We stopped for the night near some black tents at La Ne Pa, and tried to exchange my horse, but they did not want it. The Chinese merchants from Han Chong and Chen Tu came along with yaks carrying tea. Noga got four yaks to carry our loads. Made tea with snow, no water being handy.

November 13.—Yaks go very slowly. We did not get far, although on the move till sunset. Set up our tents near the Chinese merchants. They have no tent, but pile up the bricks of tea, thus making a wall to keep out the wind.

November 14.—The road very bad, horses quite knocked up. My poor old red horse, though carrying no load, could go no further, and just lay down and died. The dog also is missing. We started at sunrise, and it was sunset when we encamped. Made tea with ice.

November 15.—Over another pass. We had just descended when my little white pony lay down under me, quite done up. I had to take another.

Our party is enlarged by three lamas who are going on foot to Lhasa. Each has a pack on his back. In the evening one reads some prayers, the others joining in. They are all three very thin.

A strong, cold wind in the evening made it difficult to put up our tents.

November 16.—We had to cross a mountain which tried our tired horses severely. The ranges

LAMA WORSHIP.

are great masses of bare rock and most grotesque in shape. As we were getting ready to start, ten armed men were seen on the other side of the river. Three crossed over. We quietly got our packs on the horses. They came up to the Chinese merchants and spoke to them. We went on in front. One followed us. Two more crossed the river, joining the other two. They eyed us very much, and we feared they were brigands. Our party had only three guns; but God would, I knew, make all end for the best. The bitter wind got up again in the afternoon.

Although my horses are all knocked up, Noga will not give them barley-flour, which he gives to his own horses. I gave out some tea for the little white pony. Noga took half of it, and gave it to his pony. He takes everything.

November 17.—The way lay downhill, and the climate got much milder. There was even green grass. My black pony went on with difficulty. We came at about two o'clock to a temple, Pang Gen Gumpa. The yaks all left their loads there, and we had to put the things on our tired horses. The way led by a river with high rocky mountains on the other side. The hills were covered with bushes and stunted pine-trees. It was getting on in the afternoon when we reached the encampment.

After he had put the tent up Noga told Penting that he would not go on to Lhasa with me, but that Penting might go on and Pontso. Penting told him that we would return to Ke Gu, where the Chinese mandarin lives. He raged and swore, and said that I must go on. I then told him that I was returning, as we thought it best to go back and take another route; but I did not tell him that. He said that if that was the case, as he was leaving quite early in the morning, if I wanted anything, I must take it. I told him I wanted half the food, and a vessel to cook it in, as well as some other things. He told me to fetch something to put the flour and barley-flour in. When I returned, he said that he would kill Pontso and me, and, taking up a copper pan, he threw it at me and tried to get out his sword. Penting held him, and made for the Chinese merchants' camp, calling them to come. The chief came, and another; but Noga entered my tent and took all my things, saying that if he did not kill us he himself would be beheaded. Penting meanwhile

TIBETAN SWORD, SCABBARD, AND TINDER-POUCH.

ran away; but, when the Chinese told him to watch, and report what Noga did, he returned.

The Chinese took Pontso and me into their tent, and said that next day they would speak to Noga and get him to give me my things. They gave us mats, and we lay down to sleep.

November 18.—The merchants spoke to Noga, and he said that if I did not give him his wages he would keep everything. He was very abusive, telling them to leave me alone and that it was no business of theirs. They said it was their duty to protect us. He showed them the agreement signed in the Mongol encampment; but, as they could not read Tibetan, he made it out to be quite different from what it is.

The merchants sent for the chief of the district, and he is coming to-morrow. Pontso and I are to stay in the merchants' tent, they giving us food.

Noga had a revolver which I gave him the money to buy. Unknown to me he wanted to sell it to the Chinese merchants, and they had it in their possession, which is a good thing. I made them a present of it. God will take care of us, and has indeed raised us up friends in need.

"Better has he been to me far than my fears."

He will undertake for us. He has sent me on this

journey, and I am his little woman. He will protect me.

In the afternoon Pontso called me aside, and said that Noga is telling the people that I am English, and that to-morrow, when the chief comes, they will tell him, and then Noga and Penting and Pontso will all suffer; that he will beat or perhaps kill them for bringing me here; that the best thing would be to go on together for another day, and then Penting would kill Noga and say the robbers had done it; for, if he did not, Noga would have Penting's wife and children punished. To save them, he must be killed.

I told him that I would never consent to the taking of life, and that God would save us all, that we were in his hands. Our Father will save the two Tibetans and me. "What time I am afraid, I will trust in thee."

In the evening, after Penting had spoken to Noga, he and Pontso begged me to go back to my tent. I went back, the Chinese and the chief accompanying me. Penting, while they were talking to Noga, carried back my things.

November 19.—All went well for a time. But early in the afternoon Penting told me Noga had looked through all my things, and said that I must sell them, that if I did not there was no money to pay for the yaks to carry our loads, and our horses could not take them. I went to the Chinese merchants, and explained that the things I have would not sell for more than five ounces of silver, which I should need to buy food for myself; and, if I had to sell them now, how could we go on to Lhasa?

Poor Pontso, fearing another row, gathered his clothes together and made for the road. Penting ran after and stopped him. Both stood a long way off on the hills. The Chinese called the chief, whose tent is near, and he went with me to fetch them back. He afterwards spoke to Noga. They made me a present of butter and two fore-quarters of mutton. They were most kind.

November 20.—The horses are in so bad a condition that the Chinese will not take two in exchange for one. I went to them and asked them to do so, but they found it would not pay. However, they spoke to the chief, and I think he will give me one. He is a lama.

I have got so thin and am so exhausted that it looks as if I could not go on without a good horse. God will provide one for me. Pontso has been crying to-day. We expect to start to-morrow.

The chief gave me some butter and other things.

November 21.—Before we started, the chief let me have a good horse in place of two of my bad ones, for he pitied me, as I am not strong enough to walk. God will remember him for all his kindness.

We went through a deep gorge with perpendicular rocks on both sides. Three women who are on their way to Lhasa, tramping it with packs on their backs (one of them carrying a little baby four months old in her bosom), have joined our party. The women here wear their hair in a fringe, but plait it round the forehead. They are much fairer than those I have seen before.

November 22.—The rock scenery is very grand, but the mountains are trying. We have been crossing mountains all day.

The chief, who is with us, takes great care of me, getting his men to give me hot water for tea, and making a fire for me to get warm by. It is such a treat after the rough way I have been treated by Noga, who will not let Pontso warm water for me.

In the afternoon Erminie rode beside the chief and told him that I was English; so in the evening, after we had pitched the camp, he spoke to Noga about it. Noga shouted at the top of his voice that I was English and that after to-morrow he would go no further with me. He used a lot of abusive language. I left it all with Jesus, and had perfect peace.

The chief said that, as I was a woman, Noga must not leave me.

November 23.—The chief is as kind as ever, and does all he can for me. The road was a little better to-day. The soil in many places is red, which, with the rocks, makes a pleasant change to the eye. The valleys are narrow and the mountains precipitous. We camped by a stream. The chief will not let Noga leave me till we come to a temple two days further on. The people gave me butter and cheese.

November 24.—We have changed yaks, and the chief has gone another road to sell tea, but he has given the man with the yaks charge. He is to take care that Noga does not harm me. The three women pilgrims are still with us.

We crossed the Ber Chu Luen. Noga says he will go on with me if I will promise him one hundred taels. I told Penting and Pontso that after his trying to kill me I could not do so, that if he went with me my people would be more inclined to punish him than to reward him. Pontso begged me to agree, and said that Noga would kill us both if I refused. He was angry, and threatened to run away in the night. But last of all he broke down, and said that whatever happened he would not leave me.

November 25.—I prayed much in the night that God would save us and make Noga leave. I could not sleep for the cold. In the morning Noga came and asked me for the passport and for the agreement we made in the Mongol settlement. I told him that I would give them to him if he would give me half the food, and I claimed a horse and a little mule, as well as the horses Pontso and I were riding. The other things I must leave, or else he will quarrel. He promised to give me the horse when we get to the temple. I am so glad that he is going on. God will direct our path.

The rock under foot has changed to earth—very difficult going. We have been crossing mountains all day. Passed a lot of grouse and any number of small deer. Noga and the man with us each had two shots at them, but did not kill. We have encamped this side of the temple, for the horses' sake, because there is grass. Will go on to the temple to-morrow morning.

CHAPTER VI

TWENTY DAYS IN A CAVE AT TASHILING

At Tashi Gumpa.—In a Cave, but Away from Noga.—Three Women Pilgrims.—The Big Chief Arrives.—Stopped by the Snow.—A Feast of Thirty Little Puddings.—Birds at the Cave's Mouth.—Caravan from Lhasa.—Lamas Come for a Funeral.—Noga Departs.—Miss Taylor Sells Her Tent.—Start Again.—The Open Ground for a Bed.

NOVEMBER 26.—Noga came early in the morning and tried to persuade me to go on to Lhasa with him; but I told him firmly that after his attempt to take my life I could not do so. He made all kinds of promises, but I would not listen to them. I told Pontso to find me a place in the temple to stay in, away from Noga.

Before we reached the temple we had first a high pass to go over, the O Hay La. Noga, Penting, and Pontso went on in front. I stayed with the yaks, and Erminie with the horses. When I arrived, I found that Pontso had got me a place in a cave near the monastery, while Noga pitched his tent some distance off. The yak-driver, who is very friendly, brought me all my things. In the evening the three female pilgrims came and shared our cave. Noga wants my best horse and the mule, leaving me only three horses, so they say. We have no flour or barley-flour. Begged some salt and barley-flour from the lamas. They seem very friendly.

November 27.—Noga will not be satisfied unless he gets my horse, but Penting agrees to come with me, and so I shall be able to go forward. The cave is an excavation in gravel, and the stones keep falling on us, but to be away from Noga is a great blessing. The nights here are very cold.

November 28.—Noga wants a letter in English and one in Tibetan to say that I am not going on with him. He also wants to have the passport and the agreement made in the Mongol encampment burnt. He wants the horse I ride, and the little mule, and will not give me any of the things except a little of the barley-flour and rice. I have to consent to this. Pontso and Penting got some one to write the agreement. It stated that I was going on with Pontso and Penting. It was evening before it was done.

Penting and Pontso went to see the chief lama, and gave him a little China teapot. He was very friendly, and sent me some barley-flour, a leg of mutton, and some butter. He bought a scarf from Noga that belongs to me; it was stolen from my bag.

November 30.—The three women pilgrims left to-day. They said they could not get much food by begging here.

It snowed in the afternoon. Very cold. They say it will be still colder as we go on.

December 1.—We are left with very few things, and have to use our old tin basin to cook tea and meat in; but then we have peace, and we are very thankful.

We gave the horses cheese mixed with the used tea-leaves and a little barley-flour. At present we have no meat to spare, or else, Tibetan fashion, we would give them some.

December 2.—Very cold in the snow-clouds. Though we have nothing to do but try and keep ourselves warm, it is not very easy. Exchanged the old black pony for a white one, smaller but in better condition. We tried to exchange a few other things, but got for them only some barley-flour, which was a little better than sawdust, some bad butter, and part of a sheep that had died a natural death. Still, we sold two China plates for three rupees, and so replenished our purse if not our larder.

December 3.—One of the neighbors brought some milk and jo as a present, and wanted some medicine for his daughter. He also brought the carcass of a sheep to sell for a rupee and a half. They cut the rupees into bits here when they want change. Got him to take a piece of canvass and one rupee.

After this we saw a man ride past with a flag attached to his spear. They said he was the herald of the chief. In a little while the chief himself arrived with numbers of followers. Six mules carried his personal effects, and about fifty others followed with his goods. He is a merchant as well as a lama. In the afternoon Penting went and gave him, on my behalf, a Chinese teapot and toilet-cover, a brass tea-saucer, and some currants.

He was very friendly. Penting told him that I had some things to sell, and that I wanted a horse. He also told him about Noga. The chief bade him come next day and show him the things.

December 4.—Penting took my pair of red blankets, a white counterpane, some cotton and other cloth, a Chinese brass foot-warmer, and a Chinese dish and bowl.

He told the chief that I could not walk, and that our horses are in poor condition. The chief said the things were of little value, but he would give me a horse for them all, a good horse. Penting told him again about Noga, and the chief said he would do what he could for me. He told Penting to bring out three horses, and he would get some one to take them to a place where there is grass.

Penting did so, and found that the man who was to lead them was a friend of his. The Lord does indeed take care of us.

Snowing, so we cannot go on for a few days. The mountains are impassable.

December 5.—Sunshine again. We made a feast to-day, as our prospects seem brighter. We chopped up some of our mutton, and, making a paste of flour and meat, rolled up thirty little puddings and boiled them. They *were* a treat after the barley-flour, and we much enjoyed them.

There are robins here, and sparrows, and birds they call tit. They all seem fat and tame, hopping in and out of our cave and picking up the crumbs. I find the ground not very soft to sleep on. It is full of little stones.

December 6.—Noga came and called Penting, and invited him to go to his tent and eat meat, saying that he had bought two sheep and killed them, and also that he had bought a goat and killed it and given all its flesh to his young horse, which was looking much the better for it. He wanted to know what we were going to do, but Penting did not tell him. Penting went to see the chief, who sent me a forequarter of mutton and some fresh butter and milk. He says that we had better not go on until Noga leaves, but that we need not fear Noga. In the afternoon Pontso went to pay his respects to the chief, and took him from me a plated teaspoon and a small towel.

December 7.—A caravan from Lhasa! Among the party are three townsmen of Penting's. They say there is no snow to speak of, they met no robbers, and that no officials are stationed at the crossings of the Meg Chu.

December 8.—A company of lamas has arrived. They are going to hold a festival here for five days. They have lots of yak laden with mutton, beef, jo, cheese, etc. They have been coming all day. Three women called at our cave to see me, and gave me two sacks of jo in return for white cotton thread. I also had some patients who gave me jo and milk.

The sun is beautifully warm to-day. Penting went to see the chief, who said he had heard that Pontso was trying to exchange his saddle for a sheepskin gown, and also that he was trying to sell his horse, which he, the chief, would like to get. We sent it to him. He offered to exchange it, but nothing was settled.

Penting went again to see the chief, and gave him Pontso's clasp knife. He sent me a rupee's worth of black sugar,—three lumps. Noga came in while Penting was with the chief, but he was told to come next day.

December 10.—Noga called Penting, and tried to

GOOD MORNING!
(The Tibetan Salute.)

TIBETAN CHIEFS IN SHEEPSKINS.

SENDING PAPER HORSES TO HELP TRAVELLERS.

INTERIOR OF LAMA TEMPLE. PRAYER CYLINDERS.

frighten him with all sorts of prophecies of evil if he went with me.

December 11.—In the morning Penting went to see the chief to ask what was best for us to do. He said we had better stay here a few days longer, and then go on with a petty officer who would be going home to a place about four days' journey on our road. He sent me some cheese.

While Penting was there, Noga came and gave the chief some white calico, which he had stolen from me. He wanted to borrow some money from the chief, but nothing was settled; he said that his horses were not in a fit state to go on, and that he had no food to eat. Penting told the chief that it would be better for Noga not to leave here until we are gone, and so it is to be. The chief sent me some chilis (red pepper), which will make our meat stews more palatable.

December 12.—The lamas are all busy. Their festival has begun. They look quite academical in their red gowns.

Nearly opposite our cave is a pile of stones covering a dead body, over which some of the lamas go to perform a ceremony every day. It will, I suppose, be soon disposed of in the usual Tibetan fashion.

December 13.—The subchief came in and gave us a very black lookout, telling us it would not be safe for us to go to Lhasa. Noga and Erminie have been trying to incite the people to waylay and kill us, saying that I have a lot of gold and precious stones secreted on my person. Last evening three suspicious-looking fellows came and asked when we were going, in what condition our horses were, and whether we had a gun, etc. Many others have come to ask whether we have anything to sell.

Pontso and Penting want to go back. The chief says that Noga will be leaving to-morrow. Penting and Pontso much fear that he will lie in wait for us and try to kill us. God can take care of us.

"All my trust on thee is stayed,
All my help from thee I bring;
Cover my defenceless head
With the shadow of thy wing."

December 14.—The chief advises us to go with the subchief, and has remitted his tax to the monastery of eighteen taels. He has told him to look after us, seeing how helpless we are.

The English clothes, which I brought with me from China, I must leave here, as it is not safe to carry them further.

We had the pleasure at midday of seeing Noga and his wife depart. They had five yak-loads, the little mule, and young horse, as well as the horses they were riding. I must say that I have no wish ever to see them again. The chief has given us for the things I gave him barley-flour and meat as well as covering, also a horse, and a pack-saddle. He could not be more friendly, and there is now not much to fear. We expect to leave to-morrow, and go four days with the subchief. May the Lord provide us companions for the rest of the road!

December 15.—We thought it best to sell the tent if we could, the chief saying it would not be wise to use it, as the people on the road are all thieves and would think we were rich. He bought it himself for eight rupees.

The horse the chief has given me is rather old, but very safe and in good condition. It was noon before we got off. The chief gave me a letter, but advised me not to use it much. It is easy to see that he knows I am English.

We passed the temple, a large square building different from most I have seen, and made but a short journey, soon putting up (or, rather, putting down) for the night. The wind was very cold. We had a fire and sat round it, covering our backs to keep out the wind.

December 16.—It is the first time I have had the open ground for a bed and the heavens for a curtain at night. I slept pretty well, but found it difficult to keep the wind from my head.

CHAPTER VII

FROM TASHILING TO NAG-CHU-KA

Crossing the Frozen River.—Crows Steal the Meat.—Sleeping in Holes.—Over the Hills by a Back Way.—Secrecy.—Night Travel.—Lost.—The Road Found at Last.—A Pleasant Hiding-Place.—Christmas Day.—The Pudding That Would not get Warm.—Noga's Track Discovered in the Dust.—Crossing the Sok Chu.—A Cascade of Ice.—The Cave of Adullam.—The "Anni" Cuts off Her Hair.—How we Saw the Old Year Out.—Stopped at Last!

WE did not start very early, as we had to cross the river Tsa Chu that runs by Tashi Gumpa. There was some difficulty in driving the yak over, the river being frozen except in the middle and there rather deep water. The sun shone brightly, making it much warmer. We saw a number of golden eagles and some others of a gray and black color. They were feasting on the carcass of a horse.

December 17.—The chief offered to carry some of our things on his yak, an offer which we gladly accepted. We give our horses cheese and tea-leaves made into balls with a little barley-flour. They seem quite to relish it. We had to cross the Tsa Chu several times. It runs through deep ravines.

The soil is of many colors,—red, pink, brown, green, and white. The red and pink make the sheep on the hillsides and the white horses look of a pinky complexion.

Crossing the ice is very trying to both us and the horses. My horse is much better at it than I am. The hills are low. The road lay over grass land. It is spongy, being full of pools which are now frozen. We have to make our tea by melting the ice. There is no water. Now and then we find a spring in the river-bed where the horses and yaks can drink.

Crows steal our meat off the ponies' backs. We try as much as possible to make our beds below the surface of the ground, in holes.

December 18.—The yaks, twenty-six in number, are very good at going, the horses having to hurry on to keep up with them. It snowed, but not much. Very cold. I am getting used to sleeping in the open air. Our supper is fried mutton and barley-flour, which we all enjoy, hunger being the best sauce.

December 19.—It was ten o'clock before we were off, and a little while after the yaks stopped at the encampment of the chief of Tong Mong Pim, named Zob Gay. Penting, Pontso, and I went on with the horses, but a woman called after us, as Penting thought, to take tea. He shouted back that we did not want tea (we knew that if we went back we should have to give a present, and we had nothing to give), but it turned out that she was clamoring for one of our horses for the chief!

It was late in the afternoon when we arrived at our protector's camp. His name is La Ga Ta. When we had settled down, Penting went to take him a small present. He said it would not be safe for us to proceed without an escort, and advised us to stay the next day and see what could be done.

December 20.—I made two puddings of some suet that I begged, a few currants, some black sugar, and a little flour. One is to be for Christmas Day. The cold is extreme, and sitting all day is much more trying than riding this weather.

We tried to get the chief to come with us, but up to evening it was not decided. We exchanged some cotton for cheese. It is done up in skins, and is very good. We also exchanged a little cotton-wool for butter.

December 21.—At daybreak we started, and the chief came on with us. A friend of his, a lama, joined him. We went across country, and then struck the high road which took us over the Tsa Nang Los Bu La. We camped near some black tents.

December 22.—Up before sunrise. I had a bad

night. The chief and his friend escorted us part of the way, and then turned off to the high road to tell the chief of the robbers not to molest us, as I was an "Anni" (a nun).

Meanwhile we hurried by a back way over the hills so that they should not see us. We crossed a number of streams and the Dam Chu. This country is called Dam Chong. The rivers are all frozen. There are plenty of deer and wild horses to be seen. The grass is finer and more plentiful than we have seen lately, and the hills are low, rising out of broad plains; but there is a range of high mountains in the distance covered with snow.

We three are now fairly started on our journey alone, with God for our guide. After cooking our meal at night we move on to another place to sleep in, lest the robbers should track us, having sighted our fires.

December 23.—Started at dawn. Halted at ten o'clock to cook our tea and let the horses graze. There was some difficulty in finding a secluded spot. Every now and then Pontso takes a glance round to see if any one is coming after us. We ought to have reached the high road yesterday afternoon, but up to this evening we had not sighted it. Penting says he does not know where we are. As the horses are tired, we all walked to-day. It was difficult for me, as I have lately been suffering from palpitation. I wake up in the night and gasp for breath. We are not sorry to have lost our way, as I prayed that we might do so if the robbers followed us, and so be hid behind the hills.

December 24.—Started very early, and marched along the river-bank. I knew the road must be somewhere on the left, as we had struck off to the right on the twenty-first, and had kept on this side of the river. On the other side mountains bar the way, and Penting says the road does not cross any mountains for some time yet. While I was cooking tea, Penting crossed the river on the ice and came back beaming with the news that he had sighted the road. We did not cross, but kept on our way. Saw wild horses and deer coming down to drink in places where there are springs. Each day we have to look out for springs to water the horses. In the evening we made for a spot we saw on the hills. We wanted to get above the river, and off the road, so as to be out of sight. We found it was an old Tibetan encampment, and so there was plenty of grass and jo.

December 25.—We are resting in our pleasant hiding-place. A nice Christmas Day, the sun shining brightly. I had fellowship in spirit with friends all over the world. Quite safe here with Jesus. Penting and Pontso had to go a long way with the horses before a spring could be found, and so I got tea ready for them and put the pudding on. They were very pleased; but, although the pudding boiled for two hours, it was not warm in the middle. This is a strange climate. We drink our tea at boiling-point, ladling it out of the pan with our wooden bowls, and find it not at all too hot. If we do not drink it at once, it gets covered with ice. We are very, very cold at night and in the early morning.

December 26.—Made for the road, and, on reaching it, saw in the dust the hoof-marks of horses and one little mule. Penting and Pontso are both afraid. They think it is the Chinaman Noga following us, either to kill us or to inform the Tibetan authorities that they are leading an Englishwoman to Lhasa. I feel sure that God will take care of us. "Better hath he been to us far than our fears, than our fears." We have been gradually ascending, and crossed the Tong Er Tsa Ki La without any difficulty. Later on we crossed a second pass. At its foot a road branches off to Teng Peng E Gumpa, the monks of which turn their prayer-wheels from right to left instead of from left to right.

December 27.—While we were resting for tea this morning, a large company of merchants drew near. They had a number of armed men with them. Penting asked whether they had seen any one on the road. They said that a Chinaman, with a Lhasa woman and a servant, had stopped last night at the same place they had, and had asked them, if they met three travellers, not to say that they were on in front. Penting and Pontso are much troubled. Pontso wants to return at once, but Penting to go on a little. He told me in the evening that he could not go all the way, but would have to leave me before we reached Lhasa. The Lord will care for us and bring Noga's evil intentions to nought.

A great wind. Very cold. Crossed the So Ba Ner La.

December 28.—Passed a restless night. The men kept on thinking they heard robbers. The horses have had no grass to speak of for two days, and so travel with difficulty. We crossed over the river So Chu (or Sok Chu), passing numberless springs, the ice making a sort of cascade as the water flowed and froze.

We found a Tibetan camping-ground for the night, and so got grass for the horses and firing for ourselves. The road was very steep. Penting advised me to leave the horses and go on foot from Na-Gu-Ka, but I cannot at present walk one mile, my knees being so weak and my breath so short.

December 29.—Last night, hearing the horses break loose, I called to the men. They got up and brought them back, and saw two men who had evidently been trying to steal them. The horses, frightened at their approach, had galloped off. Penting seized his spear and Pontso his sword, and for the rest of the night tried to keep awake. The thieves probably belonged to the caravan which encamped near us last night, as no *drogpa* were in sight. It was a very cold, windy night.

We have resolved to rest for a day, as there is grass for the horses and the caravan has gone. About midday the men discovered a cave in some rocks. We moved into it. It is quite a luxury to have one's head under cover in this wild, windy climate. I cut off my hair as all "annis" do.

December 30.—We are staying in our cave dwelling for another day. Noga has a friend in the chief of a robber tribe on the road ahead, and may get him to attack us. He is sure to stay a day or two at his encampment. By halting here they will think that we have either returned or gone beyond them.

A shepherd sighted us this morning, and must have taken us for robbers; for he quickly drove his sheep away. It is a very cold, stormy day, and we are thankful for our cave, although it is small. We get smoked out now and again; but, as the men say, we cannot have a fire without smoke.

They fear greatly, but are going on. Tears come into Penting's eyes when he thinks of the danger and of his wife and two little ones. God will take care of us. Our trust is in him.

December 31.—Left the cave of Adullam. We met two pilgrims, a man and a woman returning from Lhasa. They said they had seen Noga. Then we came to the Bu Chu, where last year, Penting says, Tibetan officials were stationed to stop some European travellers trying to get to Lhasa. We feared they might be there still, and were much relieved on finding they were not. The road led over a hill and then across the Bu Chu again, where we found a caravan of merchants returning from Lhasa. Noga had told them he had three companions behind; one was a Mongolian woman with a lot of gold tied in a cloth round her waist and a gold charm-box round her neck; another was a Lhasa man, and he also had a lot of silver tied round his waist. The chief of the caravan asked about this. After our meal in the evening we set off again, going a good part of the night. It was moonlight and not very cold, as there was no wind. We crossed Bo So La, and found a place to rest in some distance from the road. And that was how we saw the old year out and the new year in.

January 1, 1893.—On getting up at daybreak found ourselves not so very far from the road, and in sight of a black-tent encampment, but we had slept in peace. The wind was very cold. I got chilled riding, and then tried to walk till I could walk no longer. The men made me a fire in a sheltered place. While we were there a man passed on horseback. He turned out to be a friend of Noga's, one of the robber chiefs. This is Sa Ma Ata country, and at present they are at variance with the chief of U. The men fear greatly. The chief asked Penting to come to his camp, but we thought it best not to go. Started again; but, finding a small cave, resolved to stay there till the sun set, when the wind would go down.

Passed Tso Ang Nag, a small lake, on the banks of which was a black-tent encampment. Road very stony. We expect to cross the Sha Chu to-night.

January 2.—Made a very long descent last night, and slept by the riverside. All day going up and down large tracts of grass land. Saw a caravan in front of us encamping for the night; so we put up near a frozen stream just below them.

January 3.—Passed a very cold night. Soon after starting we saw men with guns and horses. Noga had told their chief that an Englishwoman was coming along, and they had orders to stop us. They said we must halt by a stream that was near till the chief came up. We all sat down and made tea. Pontso and Penting fear much for their lives. May God save them! Our hope is in him, and he will do it. After tea the two men were relieved by others, and in the evening their chief arrived. We had arranged that if he did not come Pontso should steal away in the night and make his way to Darjiling, taking a letter from me. The chief's coming put at end to that. He was very affable, but he kept guard over us all night with his men. There were five of them all together, armed with guns and swords. The two who first met us have been sent to Nag-chu-ka to give information of our capture to the civil officer or principal chief.

CHAPTER VIII

UNDER ARREST AND TRIAL

Under Arrest.—Before the Military Chief.—Messenger Sent to Nag-chu-ka.—All Day Sitting out in the Cold.—Arrival of the Magistrate and Another Official.—Questioned by Them.—All go a Stage Nearer Lhasa.—Trial Before Magistrate.—More Chiefs Appear on the Scene.—Trial Before Military Chief.—He Makes His Report.—Arrest of Noga.—Arrival of the Governor of Nag-chu-ka.—The Final Trial.—Start Again for the Long Journey Back.

JANUARY 4.—This morning we were taken to a place where there was better grass for the horses. It was a ride of only half an hour.

Our meat and butter are all done, and tea and barley-flour without butter are difficult to digest.

The Nag-chu-ka chief is expected on the sixth. The wind is cold. A caravan from Lhasa encamped near us this evening. A lot of people came to have a look at me.

January 5.—A military chief has arrived with a band of soldiers. He came in the early morning, and after pitching his tent, called for Pontso and asked him many questions. The story told by Noga was that he had met us on the road and forbidden Penting and Pontso to take me on to Lhasa, but they had insisted, whereupon he had hurried forward to let the authorities know.

The chief was courteous, but declared we must go back the way we had come. I had an interview with him, and said this was impossible, that we had no food, that our horses were done up, and that I could not stand the severe cold. I had been

HAT OF TIBETAN CHIEF, WITH FEATHER AND BUTTON INDICATING HIS RANK.

brought into these straits by Noga, who had taken two of my horses and had tried to kill me. He had promised we should be in Lhasa in two months, but already four had elapsed. I must see the Nagchu-ka magistrate, and lay my case before him. To return simply meant to die on the road.

The chief questioned us all. He is quite a dandy in his way, does his hair with a fringe in front and a fantastic plait at the back. This makes him look like a woman. In the afternoon he sent a messenger to Nag-chu-ka with a note, telling the chief that we had no food, and saying that I insisted on having Noga brought to justice, and wanted to see him. Penting and Pontso were surrounded by soldiers all night, but they left me alone. The chief sent us a fore-quarter of mutton and some cheese.

January 6.—I saw the chief again to-day. He is very friendly. He asked whether I made maps as an Englishman did, who had come this way and returned to Tarsedo (Ta-chien-lu). He also asked whether I had a telescope. I told him that I had started with one, but now it was in the hands of either the robbers or Noga. I persuaded him to examine my things. I find it very trying sitting out in the cold all day.

January 7.—Early this morning a subordinate magistrate arrived, and with him another official.

He first called Pontso and had a long talk with him. Then I was called. He asked me in a very brusque manner where I came from. I told him. Then, in the usual Tibetan manner, I asked him where he came from. He answered very rudely. I told him that I must have courtesy, at which he seemed rather surprised. He said that I, being English, had no right to eat Tibetan food. I told him that I was a human being, not a wild beast, and that Tibetans coming to our country ate our food.

He said I must at once return by the road I came. I told him that was impossible. I described Noga's behavior, and said I must see him and have justice done. He declared that Noga and his wife had not been to Nag-chu-ka and that no one had seen them. I said, "I do not believe that, for we heard on the road of his arrival there." I also said that chiefs in our country do not tell lies.

He insisted that Pontso was a lama, and on my asking who had told him, he said Noga; so he was nicely caught. He said they could not bring him to justice, and that I had better return at once. I asked whether there were laws in Tibet; if there were chiefs, surely there must be justice; and I must have justice. He replied there was no use in my staying, as our food would soon be finished. I said, "We have now three days' supply; to stay or go therefore differs not." I demanded justice, and to have Noga seized, and to see the chief. I had to be very firm, as our lives seemed to rest on my taking a firm stand.

The friendly military chief told us in the evening that I was right, and that next day we would all go to his camping-ground not far from Nag-chu-ka, and that they would give us food.

January 8.—We got up early, and, after tea, started, a goodly army. We had the chief and about thirty soldiers as escort. I truly felt proud of my country when it took so many to keep one woman from running away!

A very cold, bitter wind sprung up, and I was almost frozen. I got my two men to light a fire. I have no intention of being a regular prisoner; so I act just as usual. We stopped to make tea. Just before sunset we arrived at the camping-ground. Our horses lagged behind, but five soldiers stayed with us. The wind was most bitter. Soon after we arrived a tent was sent over, which the men quickly put up; and then we were protected from the wind. Some soldiers slept near us to guard us. My two men are naturally in a state of fear.

January 9.—After we had breakfasted all three chiefs paid us a visit. They were quite gracious. They brought me a present of some butter, tea, flour, and barley-flour, and said they would also give me a sheep, which would be sent next day.

The civil chief took down a statement in writing. He asked the name of my father and mother, and my father's occupation. As he is the head of his firm, I said he was a chief. My brother and brother-in-law both being in the Indian civil service, I was able to say that they were chiefs, too. I described my life in China and my acquaintance with

Noga and his wife, alleging that he had robbed and tried to kill me. I also said I could not return the way I had come, but if there was a short route to India I would go that way; if not, they might kill me, for it was better to die here than starve on the road.

MISS TAYLOR'S VISITING-CARD.

Pontso deposed that when he was a beggar and ill I took pity on him and gave him medicine and clothes, and that out of gratitude he became my servant.

Penting told the story of his employment by Noga. He said he did not at first know that I was English; but when Noga tried to kill me he found it out, and then thought it wrong to leave me.

January 10.—The sheep arrived in the morning, and Penting killed it. The two civil chiefs left early for Nag-chu-ka. The military chief paid me a visit, bringing a man (evidently from Nag-chu-ka) with him. This man tried to maintain that Noga had not been seen there, but he found it was no use telling me that.

January 11.—The wind is so strong that it blows the tent down. I washed my sleeves, so as to look a little respectable to-morrow when the big chief arrives.

In the afternoon another military chief and two soldiers arrived. They had been watching for us at Son Yong, where there is a road to Lhasa, Noga having told them he was not sure which road we would take from Tashi Gumpa. Late in the afternoon two more chiefs came with a lama. They had a large black tent pitched, and evidently mean to make themselves comfortable.

January 12.—Before breakfast the military chief called Pontso and me. We had to go with him to the large tent. No mat was spread for me; so I told Pontso to get me one. They made no place for me to sit, except below the servants,—a great insult in Tibetan eyes.

The chief in a haughty manner told us that Noga and his wife had been arrested and brought back to Nag-chu-ka, and that Noga said he had only two horses of mine, which I had given him by agreement. This was a paper he had got written at Tashi Gumpa, which I had never seen.

I told the chief that I had never seen the agreement, and the horses had been taken without my consent.

The chief then wanted to take Pontso to Nag-chu-ka that both he and Noga might give evidence.

I said that it was not the custom for a cook to give evidence in place of his master, and that if any one must go I must go, for it was my affair.

He said that Noga, being a Chinaman, they could do nothing.

I said that in that case I must stay here, and they must let the Chinese amban know at Lhasa.

The chief was very insolent, but I kept my stand. After I had retired the lama chief and another man came, and said that if the amban at Lhasa was informed they would have to give Pontso and Penting up to the chief at Lhasa, who would punish them and put them to death. I said that I did not wish for that. He said in that case we had better all at once return to China. I told him that we had no food and no tent, and that our horses were good only for a few more days. He said that the chief at Nag-chu-ka might give us a little food. I then said that the road we had come was infested with robbers. He said that for eight days they would escort us, and then we might do the best we could. I said that only meant that they would take us to the worst part of the road, and then leave us to be killed.

After he had gone, Pontso in tears begged me to return to China and not give him up to the Tibetans.

The chief called for him, and asked him to ask me what I would do, saying that if I would return they would get the two horses and the tent from Noga and give them to me. I said that if it were possible for me to return I would, but that if I had no food or horses or tent I must stay where I am.

January 13.—I spent much of the night in prayer. In the morning the chief called for me, and was far more pleasant.

He asked what we should require for the road. I said three bricks of tea, three sheep, half a load of barley-flour, some flour, two lumps of black sugar, and some tinder for lighting the fire. He then asked if there was anything else we wanted.

I said that my clothing was not warm, and that I should like a warm dress and a blanket for the night, and that I must have the two horses Noga took, and the tent and other things that he had of mine.

After he had written down the things we wanted he said he did not know whether the chief would get the things from Noga, or would give us any food, but he would ask.

I said that if he refused I must stay with my two servants where I then was, until the Chinese amban was informed about me.

January 14.—The chief left for Nag-chu-ka. The small military chief came and told us that his child was ill. He thought my requests for food, etc., very moderate.

In the morning the people were all busy putting up tents. They told us that the big chief was coming. About midday he arrived, followed by Noga and his wife. Pontso and Penting are much afraid.

The chief called for Pontso to speak with Noga about the things I said he had stolen. I sent word that a servant could not speak for his master and, that I must go myself.

A MILITARY MANDARIN.

He invited me to come. I went, and a mat was placed for me to sit on. The principal chief and the second one, a lama, were both sitting in state.

He asked many questions, and wanted to know why I had come to their country within three days of Lhasa.

I said that I wished to cross it to get to Darjiling.

He said that the Tibetans were at strife with the English, and that the war question was not settled yet, also that Noga denied having any of my things, except the horses, which he alleged I had given him.

I said I had not.

He then said that Pontso and Penting had made them over to him in writing.

I said the horses were mine, and that my servants had no power to make them over to any one else, but that Noga, knowing they feared him, may have got them to do it.

Noga was then called in, and denied having anything of mine. His wife was called, and also denied everything. I never heard such lying.

They said they would send soldiers and escort me out of Tibet.

I said, "I am English, and do not fear for my life."

They said they would send Noga and me back to China.

I said they might carry my corpse, but they would not take me against my will.

The chief favored Noga's side rather than mine. He said that Noga was Chinese, and I English, and so he could do nothing for me; but if I did not return he would have to send Pontso and Erminie to Lhasa to be tried there for bringing me into Tibet.

January 16.—I prayed much in the night that God would save us and bring us out victorious. Pontso was called and told that if I did not consent to go back he and Erminie would be sent the next day to Lhasa, that they could not get the things from Noga, and so I must go without. They told him to tell me and to bring my answer back.

I sent word that I would come myself and speak for myself.

Poor Pontso in tears asked me to save him. I told him not to fear, for if we showed any fear they would not give us the things we required. I went and asked the chief to tell me himself what he had said to Pontso.

He then repeated it, that if I did not return they would send Pontso and Erminie to Lhasa. I said: "Is this Tibetan justice? Noga has done a great wrong to me; you say you cannot punish him. To harm me personally you fear, but you say, 'Your servant who has been faithful to you I will harm, and so harm you.' You want to send me on the road with horses that cannot go, and without a tent, knowing that in a few days we shall have to stop in a place where there is no chief, a place swarming with brigands; and thus seek to get rid of me, not killing me yourself, but getting me killed by others. I can only say that if you do not help me to return I must stay where I am until the amban is informed."

The chief then spoke quite civilly, and said they did not quite know what to do.

He then called for Noga to bring his things, so as to see if there were any of my things amongst them. There were only one or two little things. The chief then offered to give me a tent. I offered him my watch if he would exchange our horses for good horses.

I told him that if I died on the road justice would come, and if I lived to return justice would come, as I would tell the chief of our country all that had happened. I asked him his name, that I might write it down—the name of the judge who had tried my case.

The chief was much more civil after this, and said he would give me the food promised and exchange the horses.

January 17.—We were called to receive the things promised. The food was not all given; one sheep was wanting, and the butter was bad. The sheepskin they gave me was a wretched one, and there was no blanket. I told them that I could not eat the butter. The tea was good.

The chief said that he would give me one of Noga's horses in place of those stolen, exchange the others, and give me a fresh one for my watch.

In the evening a number of horses were brought for me to choose from. I never in my life saw such a collection of skeletons. I said that they were worse than mine, and would have none of them.

At last, they picked out the best and asked me to take that, and said that to-morrow morning they would bring some more.

January 18.—In the morning the chief called me, and presented me with the horse I chose yesterday, also Noga's horse; and then gave me a tent, not at all a bad one, and a sheep, and some butter, in exchange for the bad stuff he had given me before.

He said we must start to-day, and the chief of the ten soldiers who are to accompany us for eleven days was presented to me. He turned out to be the friendly lama.

CHAPTER IX

BACK TO TASHILING

Recrossed the Da Chu.—The Soldier Escort Returns.—Almost Frozen.—Watching for Brigands.—*Om Mani Padme Hum.*—Arrive Again at Tashiling.—Miss Taylor a Witch.—The Lamas Retain Her Things.—The Ice on the River Gives Way.—Penting and Pontso Quarrel.—A Frightened Hare.—Deep Snowdrifts.—Creeping Along the Rock Face.—How to Find Lost Horses.—All Day in the Path of the Yaks.—A Golok Raid.—Horses Give Up, and Drop by the Way.—Two Children Buried in the Jo.—Beautiful Scenery.—Arrive at Kegu.

IT was nearly midday before we were off. On the road a big gray wolf crossed our path, and Pontso, who was walking, evidently thought discretion the better part of valor, for he at once mounted his pony.

January 20.—We again crossed the Da Chu. Snowing. Very cold.

January 22.—Recrossed the boundary between Kham and U, at the river Bu Chu, after climbing the Peh La Pass. I have thus spent twenty-two days in interior Tibet, and hope in as many months to be in Lhasa free to tell the gospel.

Climbed the Ga Ma La, a very steep ascent. Arrived again at the cave of Adullam, where we pitched our tent.

January 24.—Halted all day yesterday. This morning the soldiers came and told us some merchants were returning from Lhasa to Penting's town; that we must go on with them; and that they would return to Nag-chu-ka, as two of their company were ill and they had not enough barley-flour for the journey.

I remonstrated with them, saying that we had not enough food to travel slowly with yak, and that the chief had said they were to go with us eleven stages, but we had done only six.

They said they would give me some barley-flour and cheese so as to make the food last, but they were determined not to go on, and that they would bribe the merchants to travel quickly. So it had to be.

January 25.—We started some time after the merchants, but soon passed them and pitched our tent.

January 26.—Stopped all day. In the afternoon the merchants came on. It is no use travelling with them; so we are going ahead to-morrow, and will trust the Lord to preserve us from robbers on the road. It is always safe to trust in him. The two men at first refused to proceed without an escort, but it was clear that if we delayed long on the road we should be frozen; so they consented.

January 27.—Crossed the Dan Tan Er La to-day. Very, very cold indeed. Last year about this time, when Penting was crossing it with some merchants, one of the servants was frozen to death by the wind. As he got colder, he said, "The wind is not so great now," and laughed, but in a little time died. They just left his body by the way. My horse fell into a deep drift of snow. It was got out with difficulty.

January 28.—To-day was even colder than yesterday. Penting says it is as cold as it can be. We were all three nearly frozen. What I should have done without the tent I do not know, as the bitter wind kept up all night. I thought we should all three have been frozen. As it was, we could not sleep much for the cold.

January 29.—Lost our way yesterday in the same part of the country as when going down. After crossing the Long Chu we went up the hills instead of striking the road. It was late in the afternoon before we found it. Being in a bad district for brigands, Pontso and Penting are frightened. When we had pitched our tent, a man came along. He turned out to be the man whom our escort coming down went to and told not to rob us. He much wanted to see me, but the men would not let him. All the first part of the night they kept awake, and were thankful when morning came.

January 30.—Set off very early, and crossed the

Tsa Nong La Gu La. Got water for the horses, which had been two days without. Snow being on the ground, it does not matter so much. They suck that.

January 31.—We are keeping to the high road. Have finished our salt, and have tried in vain to buy some, although we are in the salt country.

Saw some men busy writing "Om Mani Padme Hum" on stones which they fling into the river to be carried down-stream as the ice melts. All day crossing the river La Gu Lung Go Chu. The banks very steep, in parts almost perpendicular. Very hard and trying for the horses. Passed a lama going to perform ceremonies for some *drogpa*, one of them having died. He had three mule-loads of apparatus.

After encamping at night we were joined by another lama, and two *drogpa*, for which we were very glad, as the country is full of brigands.

February 1.—Got to the river Tsa Chu, which flows past Tashi Gumpa. Decided to go there and try to recover the things I had left.

February 2.—Arrived at Tashi Gumpa.

February 3.—Penting went to the temple, we being encamped on the other side of the river. The deputy told Penting that the lamas wanted to stone us when we arrived, but he prevented them. Noga had told them that I was a witch, and could

A PRIEST ON THE PROWL.

turn stones into meat, etc., also that I wrote down where the gold and silver was in the hills.

The lamas will not give up the things.

February 4.—We are staying for another day. The deputy told Penting that we must wait until the chief returns. I said I must leave in the morning. He will not give me my things; so we will go on without them.

February 5.—We started early. The horses are in a very bad condition. When we were crossing the river, the ice gave way, and my horse fell into the water. He struggled out, breaking the ice under his feet. I managed to stick on. Afterwards, going along a narrow path, he slipped again. It was a dangerous place. Penting came to the rescue, catching hold of the horse as it was sliding down. I rolled off, but did not get hurt.

On reaching the bank of another river our best pack-horse fell twice on the ice, twisting its legs. It was pulled up with difficulty, and now can hardly walk. Penting's horse has also gone lame. To finish up the day, he and Pontso had a quarrel, which nearly came to blows.

When we talked it over at night, the men came to the conclusion that the lamas at Tashi Gumpa are getting the devils to injure us!

February 6.—About midnight we were roused by a man calling out "Ar rak, ar rak" ("Friend!

friend!"). He was a lama going to Tashi Gumpa, having been summoned to see a sick person there.

He said it was dangerous for us to encamp there all alone; that some women pilgrims had passed that way the day before and their party had been attacked, two men killed and two badly wounded. We trust God to take care of us.

Crossed some high passes to-day. One of them is called Po Den Sem Ma La. Have camped by the Bu Chu River. A frightened hare stopped still close to my horse's feet. I called to Penting, who killed it with a stone. It made a nice change in our food after nothing but mutton.

February 7.—Could not do a long stage. Camped near some black tents. One of the shepherds having lately died, they could not (according to Buddhist custom) commit any robbery for a while; so we let our horses loose to graze, knowing they were safe.

February 8.—We had not got far on the road when our pack-horse fell in a snowdrift, and we had to leave it.

We passed a sheep killed by wolves, and still bleeding. These wolves crossed a river in front of us, which Pontso thinks a bad sign, but Penting a good one. Some of the snowdrifts on the road were quite impassable. We had to go a long way round to avoid them. The Kharo La had twelve feet of snow on it. We thought we should never get over. We had to creep along the rock face. The way down lay over a small glacier. It was really a frozen waterfall issuing from under a great dome of ice. My horse refused to go on, and had to be led. I cannot walk for more than a few yards, but I can stick on the saddle, although I nearly got thrown once or twice crossing the drifts to-day.

February 9.—Last night it snowed, and was still snowing at dawn; so we are staying here for the day. We have got a little firing, and there is some grass for the horses; these we might not get if we went on. We are thankful that we crossed the mountain yesterday, as now it will be closed for some time, except for yak.

February 10.—Did not go far, as the way was made so difficult on account of the snow. It snowed again last night.

We are following the river Tsi Chu. The valley is called Tse Ko; country, Kegu.

At dark last night all the horses but one had disappeared, and the men had to go out, and found them a long way off. The one horse left was let loose, and he followed in the track of the rest, guiding them to where they were.

This morning spied some yaks coming along the road, and in a little time some merchants came up.

They said the passes were closed except for yak. We were glad to follow in their wake.

February 11.—Very difficult to get fuel.

February 12.—Still following the river Tsi Chu. A rocky valley with craggy mountains on each side. We followed all day in the track of the yak. As it was snowing, we could not otherwise have found the road.

Heard that about a thousand of the Golok people have made a raid on Ha She people and carried off seven thousand of their cattle, as well as all their food. They yearly make raids into different parts of the country. The women and big children join, as there is little danger, and plenty to be got to eat, as well as the excitement. The Chinese are unable to check them.

February 13.—Road very bad on account of the snow, and very little grass to be had for the horses, which are all more or less done up. Penting and Pontso are walking.

February 14.—Early in the morning we left the valley of the Tsi Chu, going over the hills. We crossed numbers of little frozen streams on the mountain-sides. The poor horses found it very hard. Penting's horse kept on dropping, and mine fell under me; but I was only shaken. In the afternoon we had to leave Penting's horse on the ice. It could not be got up.

Got our companions to carry our loads for us to Kegu for two rupees and one tanka (six annas).

February 15.—Our comrades number ten, and have about a hundred and fifty yaks.

Recrossed the Tan Go La. Pontso's pony quite knocked up. We had to leave it. Pontso covered it with a felt blanket, and tears came into his eyes as we moved away.

The snow was deep and the country all swamp land full of holes. We have now only three horses left.

February 16.—At midnight we heard travellers on the road calling their yaks. The Golok people are making another raid in this part of the country, although it is only a fortnight since they came before. All day along the road we have met *drogpa* fleeing with their cattle and goods.

February 17.—Recrossed the Cha Shu La. Snow very deep, nearly up to the men's waists. We could not have progressed at all except for the path made by the yak. Very tired. Encamped near an old black-tent ground. While collecting fuel, Pontso found the bodies of two little children buried in the jo. Poor little things! No Christ in this dark land.

A lama, who was turned out of the monastery of Kegu for throwing a stone at a goat which killed it (although he had no intention of doing so), came to our tent, and the men amused themselves by telling one another stories.

February 18.—Going to Kegu by another road than the one we came. The snow is deeper than yesterday. The men and horses found it very difficult. We could not proceed. Pontso in a bad humor; he finds the walking hard.

February 20.—Came to the valley of the Tsa Chu. Road very stony. Passed the remains of a sheep and two yaks that had died in the snow. One yak of ours refused to go on and had to be left.

February 21.—This valley is the best for scenery I have seen. It is narrow with high walls. Rock, grass, and bush make up the picture. The river is deep and very swift. Every now and then the water breaks through the thick ice.

As we came near Kegu, Penting went on in front to make arrangements with his sister's husband to give us a lodging. We entered the town very quietly, but found it difficult to enter the rooms, as it was so dark. They made a place for me on a raised bed of mud. A Chinaman with a Tibetan wife, has the room next to ours. They are friendly.

CHAPTER X

KEGU,[1] KANZE, AND TA-CHIEN-LU

At Kegu (or Jyekundo).—Requested to Leave.—A Friendly Tailor.—Penting Goes Home.—Returns, and Leaves for Good.—Will the Pork Merchant take us?—The Hostess Gets into Trouble.—A Bridal Party and Dance.—Leave Kegu.—Wooded Hills and Green, Gleaming River.—Crossed the Di Chu.—The Chinese Emperor's Gift of Tea.—Hot Springs.—Country Devastated by Brigands.—Sleeping on the Snow.—Crossing the Mo Ra La.—The Worst Pass of the Journey.—Halt at Kanze.—A Huge Prayer-Wheel.—The Invisible Mandarin.—A Clairvoyant Watch.—Dango Gumpa.—Ploughs Drawn by Yaks.—Flies and Fleas.—Snow Again.—Gairo Gumpa.—A Bottomless Lake.—Houses Like Prisons.—The Men Wash.—Arrive at Ta-chien-lu.

I HEAR that a man from Ta-chien-lu is here selling pork and onions, and will be returning soon. We shall be able to go on in a few days with him.

This being the fifth day of the Chinese and Tibetan new year, every one is dressed in his best. The Chinese are giving a feast to which our neighbors are going.

February 22.—Had a good many people in to in-

[1] Kegu or Jyekundo. A tragic interest attaches to this neighborhood, since it was here that poor De Rhins met his fate by a Tibetan bullet, the year after Miss Taylor's visit (June, 1894).

spect me to-day. The chief had heard of my coming, and said he did not care whether I was English or not, but he did not want his ears made to burn by a lot of talk; so he hoped I would not stop long.

He gave Penting a piece of beef and a shoulder of mutton, and some blue cotton cloth, etc. Penting is going to his home, a day's journey over the hills.

Our Chinese neighbor is a tailor. He gave a feast, and sent me in a basin of pork and beef, a Chinese dish, which I found very palatable after Tibetan food.

February 23.—Penting was up before sunrise and soon off. The pork merchant was one of the guests last night. The tailor says Penting has been selling some of my things. A hot-water bottle he sold for three rupees. As this was among the things left at Tashi Gumpa, he must have got possession of all my English clothes. It is too bad of him not to give them up, as they will be of no use to him. I find that he has stolen a lot of little things. The pork merchant says that he would not like to travel with Penting, as he is a thief. I cannot well dismiss him, but pray that he may be unable to go.

February 24.—Had a number of lamas in to see me. They did not give me very friendly looks, and all wanted to know when I am going to leave.

February 25.—The lamas still continue to pay me visits. Three Mohammedan Chinese from Sining also came. They pretended to be Mongols, and wanted me to buy one of their horses, and asked fifteen taels for it. This is too much, as it is little and old. They came here from Sining to buy wool, bringing a load or two of sultana raisins and dates.

February 26.—I have been trying to sell my watch. The highest offer is ten taels. I say that I will not take less than twenty, as the watch cost eleven guineas (fifty taels), and is in good order.

Penting returned in the middle of the day. He says his chief will not give him permission to go to Tarsedo, and that his people are greatly incensed against him for taking an Englishwoman to Nagchu-ka and then bringing her back here. He says neither he nor his wife can stay in their valley, but will have to escape some night, taking their little son with them. They will go to a black-tent settlement, five days distant. I gave him two of the horses, the old tent, the sheepskin gown, and ten rupees in silver.

He seemed very pleased, not having expected so much. Then he wept and said he did not like our going on alone. He knew a man from Kanze who had taken a European to Ta-chien-lu, and on his return had been put in prison and tortured to death.

Pontso is very frightened, but God will take care of us.

February 27.—Penting went away before dawn. He wept again, and embraced me in the Tibetan manner, putting his forehead to mine.

After he left we asked the pork merchant what he would charge to take us to Ta-chien-lu and feed us and our horse on the way. He said he could do it for forty taels of silver and my watch. The landlord wants us to leave soon, as there is a lot of talk about me here and at the temple.

February 28.—The lamas in the monastery have been casting lots to see whether I should be allowed to stay. They sent for Penting's sister, and asked her why she had given me room in her house. She said I was a stranger and a woman, and she could not do otherwise than take me in.

The lamas trouble me with their visits, and say I must not stop any longer. We are rather in a fix, not being allowed to stay and yet not able to go. The road is notoriously bad because of brigands, and quite unsafe to be travelled in small companies. Moreover, we have only one horse and very little money. But I know it will all come right, and do not fear.

March 1.—Some Kanze merchants have come here, and will soon be returning. Their chief says they will take us for twenty-six ounces of silver, but we must find our own food. We offered him twenty-two, but no settlement was arrived at.

March 2.—The merchants have raised their price. They want thirty ounces this morning, saying they fear to take me. They are Kanze men, and Kanze is a town specially bitter against foreigners. My watch will fetch only ten ounces here; so we could not accept their terms.

March 3.—The pork merchant came and made us an offer. He says he will feed our horse, provide us with two others, and take us to Ta-chien-lu for twenty ounces of silver and the watch. We shall keep clear of Kanze, and be only fifteen or sixteen days on the road. We think it best to accept. We are to have the same food as he himself, and the horses the same as his horses.

The wife of the man who was tortured came to see me. She says he got fifty ounces of silver. The traveller was a man from Sining going to Ta-chien-lu. Her husband had been to Darjiling and Calcutta, and so the traveller engaged him. When he returned, they detained him till word came from Lhasa, and then he was released. He afterwards died a natural death. So much for reports.

March 5.—We hear that the pork merchant has made an arrangement with some Tibetans to take us for twenty taels, he getting the watch. I do not agree to this. The Tibetans say they will take us for twenty taels and half the price of the watch if we like and give us good food, and take great care of us. So I got the Chinaman to return the watch.

March 6.—A bridal party has arrived, and the bridegroom is giving a dance. Our host went dressed in crimson satin with yellow fur. The dancers are mostly men, but the girls who pour out the wine for them also dance. They came and performed for my benefit. As they dance, they sing. It would be pretty if they did not shout so much.

Our horses were stolen during the night. Pontso complained to the chief, who said he would have the town searched and send letters to find out where they were. Evidently our host had a hand in it, as he does not like to have the subject mentioned. We are in God's hands. He will undertake for us. We leave to-morrow, the men carrying our few things for an ounce of silver and two rupees.

March 7.—Started early. Fell in with a Chinese merchant, who is going home after being eight years out here. He is young and pleasant. It is a good thing to have a Chinaman with us. He has two pack-horses and five men.

We stopped for the night near a temple. There is a rest-house, but no grass can be had there; so we are sleeping in the open. The men have piled up their packs and given me the best place inside. It is not cold.

March 8.—We are now in Kham. The hills are wooded and the lakes no longer frozen. Arrived at Khansar and found quarters in a Tibetan house. Some Chinese merchants live here. One of them is to join our party.

March 9.—Started early, the road skirting the mountain. Through the valley flows the Di Chu; its waters of a deep green color. We passed a lot of villages. On the left bank of the river are cultivated lands; on the right, pine-covered hills.

March 10.—All day through a forest, the pines and other trees being the largest I have seen in Tibet.

March 11.—Crossed the Di Chu. There was just enough ice to make a bridge. When there is no ice, passengers are ferried over in boats of skin. The men are glad to have made the passage without having to pay. On the opposite bank is a small house where two Chinamen are stationed. I suppose they superintend the crossing of the tea.

March 12.—Saw some wild fowl like large guinea fowl, also a rabbit-warren. A caravan of yaks loaded with tea passed us on its way to Lhasa. It is the emperor's gift to the lamas. About four thousand yak-loads go up every year to the different temples. The farmers are impressed for this service, and have to carry it free.

March 13.—The road was not nearly so good to-day. Plenty of cultivated land. Put up at a village near some hot springs. The water has a sulphurous smell, but no taste. The men washed, as it is said to be good for rheumatism. We exchanged some tea for dried grass, and gave our horses a good feed.

March 14.—Saw a large monastery, and came through several villages to-day. Put up near a town on the mountain-side.

March 15.—Climbed over a mountain covered with snow. No trees to be seen. Very cold.

March 16.—All day without seeing any villages. Formerly there were *drogpa* all along this road, but the brigands have driven them away. Camped by a few tents in a valley, snow covering the ground, which was very wet.

March 17.—Started before sunrise. It was bitterly cold. I got nearly frozen, and was very glad when the sun came up. My horse gave out. We hoped to have cleared the pass, but had to stop on this side. Snow very deep. Slept on the snow.

March 18.—Could not sleep for the cold. Crossed the Mo Ra La, the worst pass I have had. One of the horses was frozen to death going over. We saw the remains of two yaks and a horse which had dropped on the way. The sun was so bright that we were in danger of sunstroke and of freezing to death on the selfsame day. All the men had bad eyes. Some protected themselves by putting their hair over their eyes.

We had to camp early, as the horses were quite done up. It is marshy ground. The men say the swamps here are deep and treacherous, being covered with grass. Many travellers sink in and lose their lives.

March 19.—One of the horses had to be left at a black-tent encampment, the arrangement being that the *drogpa* feed it, and the owner pays them four rupees for it on his return in the summer. If it dies in the meantime, they will get nothing.

Passed by Hor La Gumpa. On the other side of the mountain is La Tunny. That pass is closed nearly all the year. Much snow to-day.

March 20.—More snow. Our road lay by the Hor Kanze River.

March 22.—Through the pine forest. Very high mountains on the right. The Kanze monastery is perched on a rock. Saw a water-mill. Put up for the night in a Tibetan inn at Rong Pu Sa. Passed the house of a wealthy and famous Tibetan whose name is Ad Do Sa Ka Sang. He gives a tanka to every lama in Lhasa once a year. His praise is sounded all over Tibet.

March 23.—We crossed a plain, and passed numberless villages and monasteries with their cultivated lands. The houses looked substantial in the distance. Some were remarkably well built, especially those of Hor Ta Ge Gumpa. The men wanted me to dismount as we went by this gumpa; but they did not, and so I refused.

We saw a lot of people turning a huge prayer-wheel. They ran round and round after one another, both men and women. You climb up to the town of Kanze from the river, which is deep and swift. One of the horses refused to go. One of the drivers, too, is sick and in great pain. We are staying in a house a short distance out of town.

March 24.—Pontso went off to Kanze to get provisions. He brought back barley-flour, beef, butter, and flour.

The sick driver died early this morning and the horse in the night. It is very cold, and snowing, although the people are busy sowing their fields with barley.

March 26.—Expect to leave here the day after to-morrow.

March 27.—Our host has gone to see a friend of his, a young married man with a small family, who had both his eyes taken out a few days ago for highway robbery.

March 28.—Pontso went three times to see the mandarin to-day. Once they said he was out in the street. Another time he had gone to the temple, and the third time he had not returned.

TA-CHIEN-LU.

ENCAMPMENT AT TA-CHIEN-LU.

The pork merchant is telling the people that I have a watch in which I can see all that goes on in their temples.

March 31.—Got away at last about ten o'clock. Crossed a range of hills. The road very bad. Have come to a small lake with a monastery at Lan Teng. Put up at an inn.

April 1.—Arrived at Da Tong. Saw some men making a new bridge over the river.

April 2.—River Kon Sa. Coal-fields and green soil on its banks. Forest of large pines.

April 3.—Came to Dango Gumpa and town. This is an important place. Some five hundred Chinese live there. The Chinese call it Chong Fu. The drivers again wanted me to dismount, but I refused. The sun was very hot. Plenty of cultivated land. The ploughs are drawn by yaks. The women wear a curious disc of silver like a little hat on their heads.

April 4.—Crossed the river. A good road on the other side. Prickly hedges and walls divide the fields. Saw fifteen ploughs all at work on one little patch of ground, evidently the chief's.

April 5.—The road joined the river again and followed its banks. Scenery very grand, the dark-green water flowing through forests of fir with hills all around. I had a bad chest cold. The weather is much warmer; there are flies and fleas. The men give us no meat, although according to agreement they were to give us meat every day.

April 6.—Saw some large rose-bushes to-day. Arrived at Tan U Gumpa, an important place. Bought eight pounds of pork for one rupee. Camped in the open, but feared it would rain. After some persuasion the women let me sleep in a shed.

April 7.—Gooseberry-bushes! Wild apricots in blossom! The corn springing up in the fields! Green grass and—leeches!

April 8.—The wind bitterly cold. Snow on the ground. My cough worse.

April 9.—Snowed very heavily in the night, but the wind has gone down and it is not so cold to-day. Passed by Gairo Gumpa, the temple of which is roofed with gold plates.

April 10.—Soon after starting we passed the house in which one of the Devezon or "living Buddhas" was born. They have built a small temple near it encircled by trees. Climbed over a pass with descent into a deep and lovely valley. The road rough with large stones. Hills covered with verdure. Half-way down the valley the road divides, a branch going east to Ru Be Ko, a place in China, and another going west to Min Yong—a place in Kham.

April 11.—Ascended another pass. At the top

is a small lake, which, they say, has no bottom. Two horses are supposed to live in its depths. The descent on the Chinese side was much steeper and longer than the climb up. Camped again in the open, making the twentieth time on the way from Kegu.

April 12.—It snowed last night. The ground here is very swampy; two of the horses fell in. The way led down a valley between high mountains. The houses of the people are built of stone, and have small windows, which make them look like prisons. Stayed in a Chinese rest-house. Saw bamboos and some sweet singing birds. We are now only ninety *li* from Ta-chien-lu. The others will not get there to-morrow, but we hope to by taking horses from here. The Chinamen and Pontso have been and had a wash!

April 13.—Arrived at Ta-chien-lu. Found some French missionaries who were very kind. They took me to a good inn kept by a Tibetan woman whose husband is a merchant.

April 15.—Left for Kiating and the coast.